"*Porcelain* is about fundamental conflicts—between races, between heterosexual and homosexual men, between differing emotional needs. Yew has said that his play isn't really about any of these subjects, but about 'loving and relationships.' Actually it's about all of them, for it's a big enough play to handle all manner of ideas."   —*Los Angeles Times*

"A crime of passion sets the stage for a gripping, gritty, graphic voice poem about alienation. Riveting writing . . . Every word and every image is as vivid and visual as the audience's imaginations allow."   —*Daily Variety*

"The crime of passion at the heart of *Porcelain* isn't based on a true story, but it feels as gripping as the latest headline."
—*American Theatre*

"Cruel and tender, [*Porcelain*] moves and it shocks."
—*The London Independent*

"*A Language of Their Own* is not written so much as it is sculpted, with the supple precision and blistered fingers of a real artist."
—*New York Newsday*

"Forty years ago, John Osborne in *Look Back in Anger* first drew attention to the secret codes of lovers. Yew's beautifully written play now suggests that the dots, dashes and pauses of that code, the words and gestures, their establishment and sometimes their erosion and final collapse, are a metaphor for the course of the affair, indeed, an allegory of love. It's a thought, and one exquisitely expressed."   —Clive Barnes, *New York Post*

"Mr. Yew exhibits a talent for using words that are plain and simple to get at love's rich complications."   —*The New Yorker*

PORCELAIN

and

A LANGUAGE OF
THEIR OWN

PORCELAIN

and

A LANGUAGE

OF THEIR OWN

Two Plays

Chay Yew

Grove Press
New York

Published simultaneously in Canada

Library of Congress Cataloging-in-Publication Data
Yew, Chay
    [Porcelain]
    Porcelain, and ; A language of their own : two plays / Chay Yew.
  –1st ed.
        p.   cm.
    ISBN: 978-0-8021-3500-1
    1. Gay men–Drama. 2. Asians–Drama. I. Yew, Chay. Language of their
own. II. Title. III. Title: Language of their own.
PR9570.S53Y486   1997
822–dc21   96-47068

DESIGN BY LAURA HAMMOND HOUGH

Grove Press
an imprint of Grove Atlantic
154 West 14th Street
New York, NY 10011

Distributed by Publishers Group West

groveatlantic.com

Contents

Foreword

I first heard Chay Yew's *A Language of Their Own* when it was presented as a reading during the Joseph Papp Public Theater's New Work Now Festival. I walked into the theater with my producer's analytical brain completely in command, but by evening's end my brain had surrendered to my heart. This play, which explores the fragility of love and the eternal wounds that come from loss, affected me greatly. Like the rib cage which protects the heart, *A Language of Their Own* possesses a muscularity of language and a command of storytelling which allows the vulnerability and deep humanity of the characters to fully explode. This play, along with *Porcelain*, as effective as they are, are but the early steps of an exciting artist's journey. In reading them, I strongly encourage you to savor their wit and wisdom, and allow your heart to be enlightened by the feelings which live in every line, and in every breath.

> George C. Wolfe
> Producer
> The Joseph Papp Public Theater/
> New York Shakespeare Festival

PORCELAIN

Alec Mapa in the East West Players production of Porcelain *(photograph by Shane Sato)*

For Glen Goei

Porcelain, produced by Mu-Lan Theatre Company, was first presented at the Etcetera Theatre Club in London on May 12, 1992. The production transferred to the Royal Court Theatre Upstairs on August 4, 1992.

John Lee	Daniel York
Voice One	David Tysall
Voice Two	Adam Matalon
Voice Three	Julien Ball
Voice Four	Mark Aiken
Directors	Glen Goei and Stephen Knight
Set and Costume Designer	Glen Goei
Sound Designer	Mike Walker
Lighting Designer	Sacha Brooks
Stage Manager	Sarah Hopwood

On a bare stage are five chairs that face the audience; they are lined in a straight row.

There are many red origami paper cranes littered about the stage floor and around the chairs. Dressed in white, JOHN, an Asian male in his late teens, sits in the middle chair. Deep in concentration, he relentlessly folds paper cranes as the audience enters the house. When the play begins, the four characters VOICE ONE, VOICE TWO, VOICE THREE, and VOICE FOUR enter from the wings and sit on the remaining chairs. All VOICES are played by Caucasian men of various ages dressed uniformly in black.

It is important that all characters, particularly JOHN and VOICE ONE, do not look at one another throughout the play unless otherwise indicated.

No music or sound effects should be employed during the play.

Scene 1.

The VOICES *come in from offstage and create London street sounds as they take their seats. They may overlap each other's lines.*

VOICE THREE: (*Sound of Big Ben striking four o'clock.*)

VOICE TWO: (*Sounds of cars honking.*)

VOICE ONE: Watch where you're walking, you fucking sod—

VOICE FOUR: (*Sounds of an underground train screeching to a halt at a station.*)

VOICE TWO: Mind the gap—mind the gap—

VOICE ONE: No. This is not Piccadilly Circus. This is Trafalgar Square. No, not Piccadilly. Fucking tourists—

VOICE TWO: Say, can you spare some change for a cuppa? 50p? Anything? Please—

VOICE THREE: *Evening Standard.* Get your *Evening Standard* here, only 30p. "Homo toilet sex murder"—

VOICE ONE: Would you be a love and fetch us a pint of lager from the pub? Bitter lager. No lime. And a pack of Rothmans—

VOICE THREE: So the bloody Paki taxi driver drove me all the way to Primrose Hill instead. You'd think that the lot of them should at least speak English or carry an *A to Z* around with them—

VOICE FOUR: Where's the fucking number 15? I'll miss *EastEnders* at this rate—

VOICE ONE: Top news this hour: A man was found dead in a public lavatory in Bethnal Green in East London today—

VOICE TWO: Police suspect murder—

VOICE FOUR: Motive has not been established—

VOICE ONE: The alleged murderer is said to be a nineteen-year-old Oriental male from nearby Whitechapel—

VOICE THREE: London Metropolitan Police is still investigating the brutal murder. Now, more from Kylie Minogue on Capital FM—

VOICE TWO: Eyewitnesses to the crime claimed the suspect was cradling the victim after the cold-blooded shooting—

VOICE THREE: The victim, William Hope, a twenty-six-year-old male from South Hackney, was shot six times—

VOICE ONE: Sources believe that he was shot by an acquaintance—

VOICE FOUR (*overlapping, gradually louder and more urgent*): The police found the suspect at the site of the violent murder—

VOICE THREE (*overlapping, gradually louder and more urgent*): The White House has no further comment on the recent civil rights rally held outside the Lincoln Memorial. In London, there's been a fatal shooting in a public toilet in Bethnal Green this afternoon—

VOICE ONE (*overlapping, gradually louder and more urgent*): Two days ago, the Bethnal Green community of East London witnessed a tragic killing. Should handguns be made available to the public? We'll answer these questions on "Good Morning London" after the break—

VOICE TWO (*overlapping, gradually louder and more urgent*): I don't think this would have happened if the police were doing their usual rounds of the public lavs, you know. Now with what's happened I don't think I'd let my eight-year-old son into any public loo–

VOICE FOUR (*overlapping, gradually louder and more urgent*): We have clinical psychologist Dr. James Christian here this evening. Dr. Christian, what do you suppose the young man was thinking when he pulled the deadly trigger last week in the public lavatory in Bethnal Green?–

VOICE TWO (*overlapping, gradually louder and more urgent*): Well, that's a very interesting point of view. Thanks for calling. The number once again is 071-449-4000, and today's topic is the recent toilet sex murder in–

VOICE FOUR: Bang!

VOICE ONE: Bang!

VOICE THREE: Bang!

VOICE TWO: Bang!

VOICE FOUR: Bang!

VOICE ONE: Bang!

VOICE THREE: Six shots.

VOICE TWO: At close range.

VOICE FOUR: A body falls.

VOICE ONE: Slumped against the urinals.

VOICE THREE: White walls with peeling paint.

VOICE TWO: Cold mosaic floors.

VOICE FOUR: A pool of red.

VOICE ONE: Everywhere splattered with blood.

VOICE THREE: Warm blood.

VOICE TWO: Red patterns.

VOICE FOUR: Flower-like.

VOICE ONE: Patterns.

VOICE THREE: Slow-moving.

VOICE TWO: Patterns.

VOICE FOUR: Sounds.

VOICE ONE: Tiny, annoying.

VOICE THREE: Sounds.

VOICE TWO: Drips.

VOICE FOUR: From leaky water taps.

VOICE ONE: The dull hum.

VOICE THREE: From the blinding.

VOICE TWO: Fluorescent lights above.

VOICE FOUR: And a boy standing.

VOICE ONE: Breathing hard.

VOICE THREE: Weeping.

VOICE TWO: Outside.

VOICE FOUR: Traffic sounds.

VOICE ONE: Wailing sirens.

VOICE THREE: The disjointed chorus.

VOICE TWO: Of staccato footsteps.

VOICE FOUR: From street pedestrians.

VOICE ONE: Hurrying home from work.

VOICE THREE: Seems distant.

VOICE TWO: Lingering smells.

VOICE FOUR: Hanging still in the air.

VOICE ONE: Gun powder.

VOICE THREE: Antiseptic.

VOICE TWO: Urine.

VOICE FOUR: Semen.

VOICE ONE: Six shots.

VOICE THREE: A body falls.

VOICE TWO: Bang!

VOICE FOUR: Bang!

VOICE ONE: Bang!

VOICE THREE: Bang!

VOICE TWO: Bang!

VOICE FOUR: Bang!

Scene 2.

In the following scene, all VOICES, *with the exception of* VOICE THREE, *take on an array of man-on-the-street characters, a different character for each line.*

VOICE THREE: Do you know what cottaging is?

VOICE FOUR: Cottaging?

VOICE THREE: Having sex in lavatories.

VOICE FOUR: Sex in the toilets? Eh—no—never heard of it.

VOICE ONE: Cottaging. Why yes, I believe that the term came from the fact that public conveniences were once designed in the style of Swiss cottages. You know the little white brick cottages with black wooden frames. Very *Sound of Music*.

VOICE FOUR: Is this *Candid Camera*?

VOICE THREE: Excuse me, sir. We're doing a documentary on—

VOICE TWO: You're that chap on—

VOICE THREE: Alan White.

VOICE TWO: BBC?

VOICE THREE: Channel Four.

VOICE TWO: Yes, that's it. My, you look a lot smarter in real life. A bit short, perhaps.

VOICE THREE: As I was saying, we're doing a—

12 |

VOICE TWO: Well, you've been doing a brilliant job, my lad. The missus and I simply love to watch your juicy news stories at ten.

VOICE THREE: Yes.

VOICE TWO: Sally, the missus, simply raves about your butch transvestite curb-crawlers story—top notch—

VOICE THREE: Eh—thank you, sir—

VOICE TWO: And the recent story? On the impact of holiday prices on Fergie? Got me tongue-tied, it did. We stay up for you, Alan.

VOICE THREE: Yes. We're here to conduct interviews for a television documentary—

VOICE TWO: And you want my opinion.

VOICE THREE: Yes and—

VOICE TWO: My, I'm going to be on telly. Wait till Sally hears about this. Me on BBC.

VOICE THREE: Channel Four.

VOICE TWO: It's still telly, isn't it? What's the topic this week, Alan?

VOICE THREE: Toilet sex, and we're wondering if—

VOICE TWO: I beg your pardon.

VOICE FOUR: Oh blimey, sure I've heard of it. Seen it even. In Notting Hill—at some of the private clubs, even at parties. There're blokes who'll have a quick shag with girls in the toilets. Yeah—I've seen it. It's really kinky—sexy.

VOICE ONE: Yeah, but I'm not sure. Once I went to the loo in Clapham Common. Yeah . . . it was in the afternoon, maybe it was evening. I went in to take a quick piss—

VOICE TWO: Cottaging? No, never heard of it.

VOICE ONE: Well, there was this geezer standing there. He's just standing there. Like he's taking a piss or something. For a long time. And all the time he was looking in my direction. Looking at me.

VOICE FOUR: I don't think it's true. The graffiti you read on the toilet walls like this bloke gives good head—meet at this place—this time. And the phone numbers. I think it's all—you know. It couldn't be—I don't know.

VOICE ONE: He kept pulling on his . . . you know . . . looking at me. Then all of a sudden, another geezer came into the loo, and he started staring at this new geezer.

VOICE TWO: Sure, I know what it is. Saw *Prick Up Your Ears*.

VOICE ONE: He's still doing the business like—and this new chap looked back at him and walked into a cubicle. And the geezer who was clocking me just walked right in after him wallop.

VOICE THREE: Have you ever participated in toilet sex?

VOICE FOUR: Piss off! What the fuck do you think I am? Fucking queer?

VOICE TWO: Yeah, I got my cock sucked off a couple times before.

Scene 3.

VOICE ONE: It's a bit fucking bright, isn't it?

VOICE THREE: That's TV for you, sorry. Right. Dr. Worthing, can you sign this release before we tape?

VOICE ONE: This is exactly the way we discussed?

VOICE THREE: As I said to you a few days ago, I would like the Channel Four news team to be first in London to broadcast the Lee murder documentary.

VOICE ONE: I don't give a fuck whether you're the first or last. I want to know if this is exactly what we spoke of.

VOICE THREE: We will say we got this interview from you after the trial.

VOICE ONE: That's all I want to know. And to protect myself—

VOICE THREE: We agreed that if you feel there's anything unethical about disclosing certain privileged information, you needn't answer the questions.

VOICE ONE: And you want me to—

VOICE THREE: Recount your daily dealings with your client, since we don't have access to him.

VOICE ONE: And the money?

VOICE THREE: One thousand pounds will be sent to you after the broadcast.

VOICE ONE: Before.

VOICE THREE: I beg your pardon.

VOICE ONE: I want the dosh before you air the piece.

VOICE THREE: This is not what we discussed.

VOICE ONE: Then I'll walk. I'm sure there are other news shows that will want first dibs on this story.

(*Pause.*)

VOICE THREE: Before the piece, then.

(VOICE THREE *hands* VOICE ONE *a piece of paper;* VOICE ONE *signs it. All this is mimed.*)

VOICE ONE: Hey, why are you looking so bloody forlorn? You'll finally get the ratings your show needs and get yourself some fucking credibility.

VOICE THREE: Can we start, Dr. Worthing?

VOICE ONE: It's your money.

VOICE THREE: Do you—I'm sorry, I'm afraid we've got you in a medium shot, and if you won't fidget so. Let's start again. Dr. Worthing, tell us about the case you've been working on.

VOICE ONE: The case I've been working on—

VOICE THREE: The Lee case—

VOICE ONE: Oh right. John Lee, the murder in Bethnal Green. Right, of course, yes—uh—I believe I was asked by the court—

VOICE THREE: You're a—

VOICE ONE: Criminal psychologist. I'm on the case to determine—

VOICE THREE: To determine whether he was sane or insane at the time of the—

VOICE ONE: The murder—yes. The defendant wasn't able to afford counsel and—

VOICE THREE: Yes, we know that—

VOICE ONE: Listen, if you know so fucking much, why are you interviewing me?

VOICE THREE: I'm sorry, Dr. Worthing. I'm just fishing for particular sound bites.

VOICE ONE: Wouldn't it be simpler for everyone here if you gave me a bloody script instead?

VOICE THERE: Tell me about him.

VOICE ONE: Well, he's just finished his A levels—waiting to go into university in Cambridge. He's nineteen—that's all I can say on the record.

VOICE THREE: Dr. Worthing, this is a rather personal question. I have some contacts in the public prosecution sector, and they tell me that you are one of the least liked criminal psychologists in the business. Some of them claim that this is possibly your last assignment given your poor track record in the recent year.

VOICE ONE: I beg your pardon?

VOICE THREE: Let me add that they also said you are unprofessional, rude, and inconsiderate toward your clients. Some even go so far as to say you drink excessively, arriving late to sessions and not even showing up at all.

VOICE ONE: I don't think this is relevant—

VOICE THREE: There are also rumors about the sexual harassment of your female colleagues and coworkers—

VOICE ONE: I have no—

VOICE THREE: According to your peers, you constantly use profanities during counseling sessions? Isn't it unorthodox?—

VOICE ONE: Yes but—

VOICE THREE: Unprofessional, irregular, and rude are the adjectives I have received from—

VOICE ONE: Oh, for fuck sake—

VOICE THREE: Exactly what I mean. Dr. Worthing, am I safe in presuming that all these allegations are true?

VOICE ONE: No.

VOICE THREE: I'm sorry, Dr. Worthing, we didn't get that.

VOICE ONE: No. It's not true.

VOICE THREE: Once again, Dr. Worthing, audio—

VOICE ONE: It's not true.

VOICE THREE: Thank you, Dr. Worthing. I just wanted to clear the air before we ask further questions about the Lee case. I have no more questions at this time. Stop tape.

Scene 4.

VOICE TWO: John standing.

VOICE THREE: In the toilet stall.

VOICE FOUR: Nervously.

VOICE ONE: Looking.

VOICE FOUR: Waiting.

VOICE THREE: A man walks slowly.

VOICE TWO: Into the stall.

VOICE THREE: Cramped.

VOICE ONE: In his late thirties.

VOICE THREE: Balding.

VOICE TWO: A trim beard.

VOICE THREE: Wears glasses.

VOICE ONE: Clonish.

VOICE THREE: They seem to be talking.

VOICE TWO: A little.

VOICE FOUR: Hi.

VOICE ONE: John nods.

VOICE TWO: The clone wets his lips.

VOICE THREE: Slowly.

VOICE FOUR: Knowingly.

VOICE TWO: John's eyes make a quick study.

VOICE ONE: Of the man's body.

VOICE FOUR: His eyes.

VOICE TWO: Transfixed.

VOICE THREE: Touching his body.

VOICE TWO: His trembling hands.

VOICE ONE: Run down the stranger's body.

VOICE FOUR: Unevenly.

VOICE TWO: Nervously.

VOICE THREE: The man holds John's head.

VOICE FOUR: And leads John down.

VOICE TWO: To his swelling crotch.

VOICE ONE: His face against the soft denim.

VOICE THREE: A faint, familiar smell.

VOICE TWO: Smells of soap and sweat.

VOICE ONE: The man's head arches slowly.

VOICE FOUR: Leans on the toilet wall.

VOICE THREE: Pressing against the wall.

VOICE TWO: The man looks at the ceiling.

VOICE THREE: Blinking hard.

VOICE FOUR: Breathing heavily.

VOICE TWO: Through his nose.

VOICE THREE: His body spasms.

VOICE ONE: Long breaths.

VOICE FOUR: Deep breaths.

VOICE TWO: Uneven breaths.

Scene 5.

VOICE ONE: Thanks for letting me smoke. I'll just fucking die if I don't—do you want a fag? Eh—I mean—cigarette.

JOHN: I don't really care for lung cancer.

VOICE ONE: Good for you. It's habit forming. I don't really have all your stuff with me. Your name?

JOHN: John—

VOICE ONE: Yes, that's it. John—John Lee. Eh—my name's Jack Worthing. Doctor—

JOHN: *Importance of Being Earnest.*

VOICE ONE: What?

JOHN: Oscar Wilde.

VOICE ONE: I don't—

JOHN: Jack Worthing is the name of a character—

VOICE ONE: Oh, that's right. The play about people pretending to be other people just to get laid—something like that.

JOHN: I auditioned for the role a few years ago in school.

VOICE ONE: Really? How nice.

JOHN: Didn't get it.

VOICE ONE: Uh-huh. Why?

JOHN: They said I didn't look the part.

VOICE ONE: Oh, I see. I'm sorry.

JOHN: I'm not. You're American?

VOICE ONE: British.

JOHN: You have an accent.

VOICE ONE: I spent many years in America. Studying. Working.

JOHN: Ah, the crow and the sparrow.

VOICE ONE: What are you talking about?

JOHN: Nothing. A stupid story my father told me when I was young.

VOICE ONE: What story?

JOHN: You and I are the same.

VOICE ONE: I don't understand.

JOHN: You'll never understand.

VOICE ONE: Right. Off to work then, shall we? You probably know what these are. Rorschach blot test cards. Pretty, aren't they?

JOHN: Very pretty.

VOICE ONE: So, tell me what you—

JOHN: See?

VOICE ONE: Well?

JOHN: I don't know.

VOICE ONE: Try. Tell me—

JOHN: Patterns—dots.

VOICE ONE: Yes—yes. But what do you see?

JOHN: I don't see anything.

VOICE ONE: Eh—let me rephrase that—what does this remind you of?

JOHN: Patterns—dots.

VOICE ONE: Well, aside from patterns and dots. The shapes. Do the shapes resemble anything to you? Anything in particular?

JOHN: Nothing.

VOICE ONE: All right, let's try another. How about this one?

JOHN: Patterns and dots.

VOICE ONE: Look here, you're not making any of this—

JOHN: Easy?

VOICE ONE: Why?

JOHN: Why not?

VOICE ONE: Can we put our eyes on this card and tell us the first thought—

JOHN: That comes into my pretty head?

VOICE ONE: Don't put words in my mouth.

JOHN: What shall I put in?

VOICE ONE: God, my fucking headache.

JOHN: Listen, Dr. Worthing, I know you are here to—

VOICE ONE: Help you.

JOHN: I appreciate your concern, but I don't need your help. Please go away.

VOICE ONE: Listen, I'm only here to do a job, not to make friends. I'm here to find out why you—

JOHN: Killed him.

VOICE ONE: In so many words.

JOHN: I'm guilty.

VOICE ONE: Let the jury be the judge of this.

JOHN: But I am.

VOICE ONE: Look—

JOHN: I am guilty of each and every shot.

VOICE ONE: Listen, John, I'm tired. I'll be honest with you since I feel we should have an honest working relationship. I'm fucking tired. I've got a fucking headache. I'd rather be in bed—

JOHN: Fucking.

VOICE ONE: Right. And you're in here for murder. It's big time, not some small, petty—

JOHN: I know.

VOICE ONE: We're talking about life here. Behind the bars, never to see the light of day, with lots of men—

JOHN: Fucking?

VOICE ONE: Men who'll slice you up for fun. Now, let's start again. So what do you see?

JOHN: I don't know. Dots—patterns.

Scene 6.

VOICE THREE: Dr. Worthing, what information did you expect to get out of John Lee through the blot tests?

VOICE ONE: Perhaps an idea of who he is and what he is. Why he did what he did. It's a kind of Tarot cards psychologists use.

VOICE THREE: Was it effective?

VOICE ONE: Not in the beginning. Perhaps he didn't trust me. Perhaps he was just being difficult. Perhaps he still hadn't recovered from the shock—

VOICE THREE: And?

VOICE ONE: Then he gradually opened up and told me things.

VOICE THREE: What kind of things?

VOICE ONE: Things. All kinds of things.

VOICE THREE: Like?

VOICE ONE: I thought you were an investigative reporter.

VOICE THREE: I am. So what did John Lee tell you?

VOICE ONE: I can't disclose that special client-counselor information to you, Mr. White. That would be quite unprofessional, don't you think?

VOICE THREE: Then how do you look at this case, Dr. Worthing?

VOICE ONE: What do you mean?

VOICE THREE: You're heterosexual, I presume.

VOICE ONE: Very.

VOICE THREE: You've never cottaged. You're definitely not Oriental. So how do you look at this case as a heterosexual white male?

VOICE ONE: It's a job.

VOICE THREE: No bias?

VOICE ONE: None.

VOICE THREE: Psychologists are, by definition, neutral and impartial to their cases. But you must have some personal opinions.

VOICE ONE: Of course, but—

VOICE THREE: And?

VOICE ONE: Look, this is getting rather—

VOICE THREE: Okay, we'll stop there. Look, just between you and me.

VOICE ONE: This is off the record, right?

VOICE THREE: Oh, definitely. It'd be unethical if we—

VOICE ONE: I think—personally, between you and me, I think this whole case is—sick. Public sex is an offense. Murder is an offense. Well, let me put it in simple words—a queer Chink who indulges in public sex kills a white man. Where would your fucking sympathies lie? Quite open and shut, isn't it?

VOICE THREE: Quite.

VOICE ONE: But I am keeping an open mind. Have to protect my client's bloody interest.

VOICE THREE: Of course.

VOICE ONE: It's just that I have nothing in common with those types, you know.

VOICE THREE: What types?

VOICE ONE: Those types.

VOICE THREE: I see. It must be very difficult for you as a psychologist to meet such a variety of types every day.

VOICE ONE: It's work.

VOICE THREE: Thank you.

VOICE ONE: Not at all. Anything for you boys at the BBC.

VOICE THREE: Channel Four.

VOICE ONE: Same thing. Say, you don't happen to have a cigarette on you, do you?

VOICE THREE: Sorry, you had the last one. (*Pause, loud whisper.*) Did we get that sound bite?

Scene 7.

VOICE FOUR: There were two big trees on a field.

VOICE TWO: One at each end.

VOICE THREE: In one particular tree.

VOICE ONE: Lived a large family of black crows.

VOICE FOUR: The crows were noisy.

VOICE TWO: Loud.

VOICE THREE: Greedy.

VOICE ONE: Clumsy.

VOICE FOUR: Unwieldy.

VOICE TWO: Across the field was another tree.

VOICE THREE: A family of sparrows.

VOICE ONE: Chirpy.

VOICE FOUR: Merry-making.

VOICE TWO: Graceful.

VOICE THREE: Happy.

VOICE ONE: Beautiful sparrows.

VOICE FOUR: One particular crow always saw them.

VOICE TWO: Always studied and observed them.

VOICE THREE: The lonely crow looked at them.

VOICE ONE: With such longing.

VOICE FOUR: Longing to sing happy, chirpy, little songs with them.

VOICE TWO: Longing to fly in fanciful formations.

VOICE THREE: Climbing up, plunging down, bursting free.

VOICE ONE: Soaring heavenwards like a magnificent paper kite.

VOICE FOUR: Swooping earthwards like a thunderous ocean waves in a Japanese watercolor picture.

VOICE TWO: The crow made up its mind.

VOICE THREE: Packed its bags.

VOICE ONE: Bade a tearful farewell to its surprised family.

VOICE FOUR: Flew clear across the field.

VOICE TWO: To the tree of singing, happy, chirpy, beautiful sparrows.

Scene 8.

VOICE ONE: What are you doing? You're folding something.

JOHN: Very observant.

VOICE ONE: Paper birds.

JOHN: Origami.

VOICE ONE: Pigeons?

JOHN: Do they look like pigeons?

VOICE ONE: Sparrows, then.

JOHN: No.

VOICE ONE: Crows? I don't know.

JOHN: Cranes.

VOICE ONE: They're—interesting. Why are you folding so many of them?

JOHN: For fun.

VOICE ONE: Come on, why are you folding them?

JOHN: It's something you wouldn't understand.

VOICE ONE: I might.

JOHN: You won't.

VOICE ONE: How do you know I won't.

JOHN: Tradition.

VOICE ONE: What tradition?

JOHN: Japanese tradition.

VOICE ONE: But you're Chinese.

JOHN: So?

VOICE ONE: What's the tradition?

JOHN: Dr. Worthing.

VOICE ONE: Jack, please.

JOHN: Dr. Worthing, let's not get too chummy and pretend you're interested in my life, because you aren't.

VOICE ONE: I am interested. The Oriental culture has always—

JOHN: Fascinated you?

VOICE ONE: Yes.

JOHN: How nice. What part of our Oriental culture so fascinates you, Dr. Worthing?

VOICE ONE: I like Chinese food.

JOHN: Is it our obedient and subservient geisha girls? Maybe our suntanned go-go girls who'll fuck you for less than five pounds in Bangkok? Or is it our ancient Oriental erotic acts? Maybe *The King and I? Miss Saigon? Suzie Wong?* Which is it, Dr. Worthing?

VOICE ONE: All those actually, but five pounds a shag sounds reasonable to me.

JOHN: Dr. Worthing, did it ever occur to you that your fascination is rooted in ignorance? Like everyone else—

VOICE ONE: Who's everyone else?

JOHN: Like everyone else you sit comfortably on the other side of the wall. Perched. Watching us. Studying us. Looking at us. And you never once leave the other side to join us or understand us. You don't want to. We are mythicized by you. We are your interesting geisha girls, bespectacled accountants and dentists, your local Chinese takeaway. Your fascination. And why should you want to climb over and join us? Are you afraid of finding out that we're just the same as you? Have the same feelings and the same fears as you? How we are so much alike? You and I?

VOICE ONE: You must think you're very clever.

JOHN: Enough to detect a stiffening in your voice.

VOICE ONE: It's a very good guess.

JOHN: Nevertheless, a very accurate one, Dr. Worthing.

VOICE ONE: You're full of shit—

JOHN: And you're pathetic—

VOICE ONE: No little queer is going to tell me—

JOHN: My, my. Such unattractive and unprofessional language. Enough to get you dismissed from my case and perhaps from a rosy future in the criminal psychology profession. Who'll have to pay for your excessive cigarettes and lager habits then?

VOICE ONE: Listen, you lousy homo Chink—

JOHN: I think we've already established the fact that I'm a homo Chink, Dr. Worthing. (*A pause.*) I presume your silence indicates that this session is over. Do drive safely. Clear skies can be deceiving.

Scene 9.

VOICE THREE: Inspector Piper, what can you tell me about the murder that took place here about a month ago?

VOICE FOUR: There was some commotion in the public convenience by the Bethnal Green tube station. I was dispatched to the area to investigate the case.

VOICE THREE: What did you see when you got there?

VOICE FOUR: There was a crowd of people milling outside the toilets. Some of them were hysterical. They claimed they heard gunshots inside. The victim and the accused were lying in a pool of blood. Mr. Lee seemed to be holding Mr. Hope in his arms, rocking him, like a baby. Mr. Hope had blood all over his head and chest, and Mr. Lee was just holding him.

VOICE THREE: What did you know about this toilet in Bethnal Green?

VOICE FOUR: Nothing much.

VOICE THREE: Let me put it this way: Have you heard anything peculiar about this particular toilet before?

VOICE FOUR: No. Should I?

VOICE THREE: Do you feel John Lee is the killer?

VOICE FOUR: Mr. White, I don't know all the facts surrounding the—

VOICE THREE: You don't need facts. Given what you saw, do you think John Lee is guilty?

VOICE FOUR: I don't know.

VOICE THREE: You are a police inspector. You walk into the public lavatory, you see two men—one dead, and the other living, with a gun by his side. What was your first instinct?

VOICE FOUR: From what I saw, the accused was mourning, like he was a friend.

Scene 10.

VOICE ONE: So how are you today?

JOHN: In prison. And you?

VOICE ONE: Are they treating you well here?

JOHN: I am tired.

VOICE ONE: How well?

JOHN: It's not exactly Buckingham Palace.

VOICE ONE: You have everything you need, I presume.

JOHN: My own cell. My own shower.

VOICE ONE: Good. Anything else?

JOHN: All the prisoners here look at me very strangely.

VOICE ONE: What do you mean "strangely"?

JOHN: In the valley of the blind, I'm the one-eyed man.

VOICE ONE: Meaning?

JOHN: They know I'm getting special treatment.

VOICE ONE: How?

JOHN: For a psychologist you ask a lot of stupid questions. Dr. Worthing, you should learn to open your eyes. Because I am different from the rest.

VOICE ONE: You're an alleged murderer.

JOHN: And?

VOICE ONE: And you're gay.

JOHN: Always been the case, hasn't it? Separate from the rest of the world. Even in prison. I'm not sure if I should be grateful in this instance.

VOICE ONE: What else have you been doing?

JOHN: Giving the warden intense blow jobs.

VOICE ONE: What else?

JOHN: Reading.

VOICE ONE: Reading what?

JOHN: A book.

VOICE ONE: What is the book about?

JOHN: The history of Chinese art.

VOICE ONE: Oh.

JOHN: It's either that or cowboy novels with half the pages missing.

VOICE ONE: I can bring you another book the next time.

JOHN: No. Thanks.

VOICE ONE: Good book, is it?

JOHN: Why are you so interested in making small talk?

VOICE ONE: Can't I be friendly?

JOHN: You have ulterior motives.

VOICE ONE: Why are you so defensive?

JOHN: Am I? I thought I was offensive.

VOICE ONE: How far have you gotten? In the book, I mean.

JOHN: You'll find me under Chinese porcelain.

VOICE ONE: First made by the Chinese.

JOHN: Very impressive, Dr. Worthing.

VOICE ONE: I do have that fascination, you know.

JOHN: The fascinating thing about porcelains is the process. Coarse stone powders and clay fused by intense temperatures to create something so delicate, fragile and beautiful. Two extremes, two opposites thrown together only to produce beauty. Like the fairy tale—*Beauty and the Beast*.

VOICE ONE: That's a fascinating—eh, interesting analogy. Let's take this a little further. Who do you see yourself as? Beauty or the beast?

JOHN: What do you mean?

VOICE ONE: In the context of the whole incident. In Bethnal Green. Do you see yourself as Beauty or the beast?

JOHN: What do you see me as?

Scene 11.

JOHN *covers his face with his hands. All the* VOICES *are looking at* JOHN, *taunting him, at first softly then gradually louder, like a shout. As the scene progresses, the* VOICES *get up and surround* JOHN *in a claustrophobic semicircle and yell at him.*

VOICE ONE: Queer.

VOICE THREE: Chink.

VOICE FOUR: Poof.

VOICE TWO: Slit eyes.

VOICE ONE: Queer.

VOICE THREE: Chink.

VOICE FOUR: Cocksucker.

VOICE TWO: Slit eyes.

VOICE ONE: Queer.

VOICE THREE: Chink.

VOICE FOUR: Ugly.

VOICE TWO: Homo.

VOICE ONE: Queer.

VOICE THREE: Chink.

VOICE FOUR: Go away!

VOICE TWO: Chink.

VOICE ONE: Queer!

JOHN: No.

VOICE THREE: Chink!

VOICE FOUR: Go back to China!

VOICE TWO: Slit eyes!

VOICE ONE: Queer!

VOICE THREE: Homo!

JOHN: No.

(VOICES *begin to overlap and yell.*)

VOICE FOUR: Go back to Hong Kong!

VOICE TWO: Six shots.

VOICE ONE: Slit eyes!

VOICE THREE: Queer!

VOICE FOUR: A body falls.

VOICE TWO: You don't belong here!

VOICE ONE: Homo!

VOICE THREE: Chink!

VOICE FOUR: Bang!

JOHN: No.

VOICE TWO: Bang!

VOICE ONE: Queer!

JOHN: No.

VOICE THREE: Bang!

VOICE FOUR: Slit eyes!

JOHN (*louder*): No.

VOICE TWO: Bang!

VOICE ONE: Chink!

VOICE THREE: Bang!

JOHN (*louder*): No!

VOICE FOUR: Homo!

VOICE TWO: Bang!

JOHN (*screams*): No!

Scene 12.

VOICE ONE: How about this one?

JOHN: Well, it—it does look like a flower.

VOICE ONE: Orchid? Daisy? Daffodil?

JOHN: A poppy. A red poppy.

VOICE ONE: Where did you see this red poppy?

JOHN: I don't remember.

VOICE ONE: What do you feel when you see this card?

JOHN: Sadness. A certain sadness.

VOICE ONE: I see.

JOHN: Yet, warmth.

VOICE ONE: Who do you see in it?

JOHN: Will.

VOICE ONE: William Hope?

JOHN: Yes.

VOICE ONE: What about him?

JOHN: Don't know. Just him and the red poppy.

VOICE ONE: We haven't spoken about William Hope.

JOHN: There's nothing to speak of.

VOICE ONE: Tell me something about him.

JOHN: He's dead.

VOICE ONE: What else?

JOHN: Surely, you must have a folder on him.

VOICE ONE: Yes, but I want to hear it from you.

JOHN: I don't want to talk about him.

VOICE ONE: Do you miss him?

JOHN: Why should I?

VOICE ONE: Shouldn't you?

JOHN: I don't miss him.

VOICE ONE: Really? It says in my folder that the two of you were involved in some capacity.

JOHN: That's correct.

VOICE ONE: Sexually?

JOHN: Yes.

VOICE ONE: I see.

JOHN: Tell me what you see, Dr. Worthing.

VOICE ONE: Only what you want me to see.

JOHN: So we're playing little mind games, aren't we?

VOICE ONE: You are. I'm not.

JOHN: This is all a trick, isn't it? Reverse psychology.

VOICE ONE: Whatever you say.

JOHN: Surely a leopard cannot change its spots.

VOICE ONE: As I said before, I have a job to do. I am here to help, if you want me to. If you don't, I'll try and do my job all the same.

JOHN: You're no fun.

VOICE ONE: Murder isn't fun.

JOHN: It can be.

VOICE ONE: Do you regret killing William Hope?

JOHN: No.

VOICE ONE: Why?

JOHN: Because he deserved it.

VOICE ONE: Do you miss him?

JOHN: You're repeating yourself, Dr. Worthing.

VOICE ONE: Well, do you?

JOHN: I don't—that's why I killed him.

VOICE ONE: Why did you do it?

JOHN: Because I hated him.

VOICE ONE: You hate him.

JOHN: Yes.

VOICE ONE: Really hate him.

JOHN: Yes.

VOICE ONE: How much do you hate him?

JOHN: Why are you asking me this question over and over again?

VOICE ONE: Just wanted to make sure. How much do you hate him?

JOHN: I don't know.

VOICE ONE: Hated him so much you murdered him in cold blood?

JOHN: Yes.

VOICE ONE: Hated him so much that you shot him six times.

JOHN: Yes.

VOICE ONE: Not one shot but six.

JOHN: Yes. Six.

VOICE ONE: Six shots. Two in the face. One in the throat. Two in the chest and one in the groin.

JOHN: Yes.

VOICE ONE: Six shots.

JOHN: I'm tired.

VOICE ONE: Six shots.

JOHN: Yes! What do you want from me?

VOICE ONE: Just the truth.

JOHN: I miss him.

Scene 13.

VOICE THREE: You said you had toilet sex before.

VOICE TWO: Yes. With a lot of men. A lot of men.

VOICE THREE: How many men?

VOICE FOUR: Can't say for sure.

VOICE TWO: Lost count after thirty.

VOICE THREE: Tell me about your experiences.

VOICE TWO: Ohhh, wouldn't you like to know, honey?

VOICE ONE: Are you sure no one will recognize me on television?

VOICE THREE: Why do you do it?

VOICE TWO: You know, that's a question I keep asking myself. I don't know. There's a strange kind of attraction to it. Kind of excitement.

VOICE THREE: What kind of excitement?

VOICE TWO: Sexual excitement. A certain kind of anonymity. It's like an exclusive ritual, a gentlemen's sex club.

VOICE ONE: I wouldn't go, but my wife doesn't like to kiss it.

VOICE FOUR: My girlfriend sucks like she's—she just doesn't do it the way I like it.

VOICE TWO: It's convenient. Like a supermarket. It's there. You walk in, get it, and go home. You don't even have to make small talk, buy him a lager, or exchange phone numbers you know they'll never call.

VOICE FOUR: Those queers there like to suck cock—and they do it good. So I'm just obliging them. Could say I'm doing my bit for gay rights, you know what I mean? (*Laughs raunchily.*)

VOICE ONE: I think there's an element of danger to it, too—an element of being discovered. And that's why people like to fuck in parks, back alleys, toilets, offices, and planes. Don't you?

VOICE FOUR: No, I'm not being unfaithful to my girlfriend. I mean, I think being unfaithful to my girlfriend is having sex with another woman.

VOICE ONE: I'm not bisexual, no.

VOICE FOUR: My lover and I have a very open relationship.

VOICE ONE: I don't think there's much cottaging going on anymore, especially when most of the public lavs are shut down and there's always an attendant there. Not anymore. Cottaging went out with disco.

VOICE FOUR: I don't know why there's cottaging. Maybe it has to do with the boarding school system or something.

VOICE TWO: You'll simply have to die when you hear this. I got sucked off by an Anglican priest. Swear to God. See, he preaches in my parish. Didn't recognize me. What a lark! Never thought they'd take the get-down-on-your-knees thing quite so seriously.

VOICE THREE: How old were you when you first had this experience?

VOICE FOUR: About seventeen, and it happened in a shopping center in North London. Whitelands.

VOICE TWO: Yeah, once I got fucked in the toilet by this blond Adonis. It was a good fuck. Safe sex, of course. My arse just tingles when I think about it. Oh, can I say that on television?

VOICE ONE: It's really unsafe nowadays to be doing toilets. This thing with AIDS is quite frightening. Who knows what type of people are in there?

VOICE FOUR: I know you can't get it from sucking, but who knows?

VOICE THREE: If there weren't AIDS, would you do the toilets?

VOICE FOUR: If the coppers weren't snooping about, maybe.

VOICE ONE: Yeah, why not?

VOICE TWO (*airily and in a camp voice*): Not anymore. This girl needs a spring mattress, a down pillow, and the West End soundtrack of *Camelot* before she can do the wild thing. (*He snaps his fingers in a dramatic way.*)

Scene 14.

VOICE ONE *gently touches* JOHN's *shoulder.* JOHN *notices his touch but says nothing.*

VOICE ONE: I know what you're feeling.

JOHN: You don't know what I am feeling. Stop trying to say something you don't mean. How can you possibly know what I'm feeling?

VOICE ONE: Because I've lost someone, too. She didn't die, but a loss is a loss.

JOHN: We're not in the same situation.

(VOICE ONE *returns to his chair.*)

VOICE ONE: Let's get back to the cards. This reminds you of a red poppy. Somehow you're reminded of William Hope. When did you first meet him?

JOHN: Two—no, three—months ago. January.

VOICE ONE: Where?

JOHN: I don't want to talk about him.

VOICE ONE: Why not?

JOHN: I just don't want to.

VOICE ONE: There must be a reason.

JOHN: I don't have a reason, just a feeling.

VOICE ONE: Of?

JOHN: Pain.

VOICE ONE: You can get rid of this pain by talking about it.

JOHN: I know. But somehow—I like this pain—I need it.

VOICE ONE: Where did you meet William Hope?

JOHN: In a public toilet.

VOICE ONE: Which one?

JOHN: That one.

VOICE ONE: Bethnal Green?

(JOHN *nods*.)

VOICE ONE: And?

JOHN: I was sitting in the cubicle.

VOICE ONE: Cubicle doing what?

JOHN: Waiting.

VOICE ONE: Waiting for what?

JOHN: Waiting.

VOICE ONE: I see.

JOHN: It was late afternoon—cold—

(VOICE FOUR *plays William Hope character*.)

VOICE FOUR: About four-thirty, five— Since work was quiet that day, I decided to knock off early and thought I'd make a quick trip to the loo—you know—before going home.

JOHN: Things were quiet that Thursday—

VOICE FOUR: I don't know why, but I went into the lav at Bethnal Green— Guess I live close by, and I've been there before and some chappies got me off.

JOHN: And Will came in—

VOICE FOUR: I went in—thinking, you know, that someone might be there. There's always someone there—if there isn't—you wait. Things do happen, you know. They usually do.

JOHN: At first I thought he was just going to take a piss— Then he started to walk around the toilet. I just kept still in my cubicle—hearing his footsteps.

VOICE FOUR: At first I thought there wasn't anybody there. It was pretty quiet. So I started to check out—

JOHN: He started to walk by the cubicles—really slowly—deliberately. I don't know why, but I was anxious—my heart is beating away—I mean, I've done this before, but I always get—anxious. And—then he passed mine—my cubicle and—he stopped. He wasn't handsome, but he was—attractive. Dark hair, dark eyes. Something magnetic about his features—almost rough yet—gentle. Though he stood in front of my cubicle for a few seconds, it seemed like an eternity.

VOICE FOUR: There was an Oriental bloke—Chinese, Japanese, or something looking at me. He's—not bad looking—looks like any other Chink, I guess—

JOHN: He smiled.

VOICE FOUR: He just kept looking—just sitting there—and I wasn't in the mood to play the usual cat-and-mouse games, so I nodded to him.

JOHN: And I nodded. He came into the stall, and we started looking at each other. He shut the door gently behind him—all the while he kept staring at me. It was arresting.

VOICE FOUR: I've never got it off with an Oriental before, you know. They're not my type generally. But there wasn't anyone else around, and a mouth is a mouth. And it looks as if he has never done it before. Could be an act, for all I know—the innocent puppy dog look. He looked so—what's the word? Fragile? Yeah. Fragile. I touched his face.

JOHN: His rough, warm hands touched my face, my head—and he pulled me close—to his crotch—

VOICE FOUR: And rubbed his face around it. I was about to burst in my jeans. My hands cradling his soft, black hair. Then he—

JOHN: Unzipped his jeans and took it out. Hard.

VOICE FOUR: It was a warm feeling. Nice.

JOHN: It was—

VOICE FOUR: Good—good—

JOHN: Yes—good—

VOICE FOUR: Yes—yes—yes—yes—slow—slow—

JOHN: Hmm—slow—

VOICE FOUR: Hmm—yeah—oh god—oh god—

JOHN: He came over my shirt.

VOICE FOUR: In powerful spurts.

JOHN: Warm and sticky.

VOICE FOUR (*breathing heavily*): That felt good. Felt really nice. It was—

JOHN: Beautiful.

VOICE FOUR: A great blow job.

JOHN: It was—beautiful.

VOICE FOUR: I mean, don't get me wrong. I'm not a queer or anything, but like the other boys I like to—get off. It's just a physical thing, you know. It's just sex.

VOICE ONE: There, wasn't that simple?

JOHN: I feel so—

VOICE ONE: Vulnerable?

JOHN: I don't like to be—

VOICE ONE: I know. None of us do.

JOHN: I know where I remember seeing the picture of the red poppies. Will has this print that quite looks like that. He hangs it by his bed.

Scene 15.

VOICE THREE: Mr. Lee? You're Mr. Lee, aren't you? Excuse me, Mr. Lee?

VOICE TWO: I am no Mr. Lee. Wrong person.

VOICE THREE: But I spoke to—

VOICE TWO: I no Mr. Lee. I no Mr. Lee.

VOICE THREE: Mr. Lee, I'm Alan White from Channel Four, perhaps you've seen me on—

VOICE TWO: Go away.

VOICE THREE: Mr. Lee, we're doing a special documentary about your son's—

VOICE TWO: Please. Please go away.

VOICE THREE: Mr. Lee, have you anything to say about your son's arrest last week?

VOICE TWO: Don't know what you say.

VOICE THREE: Your son who was—

VOICE TWO: No son.

VOICE THREE: There was a fatal shooting in Bethnal Green—

VOICE TWO: No son.

VOICE THREE: Aren't you the father of John Lee?

VOICE TWO: I have no son.

VOICE THREE: But my—

VOICE TWO: No son.

VOICE THREE: Are you—

VOICE TWO: I have no son! I have no son!

VOICE THREE: Mr. Lee?

VOICE TWO: No son! No son! My son is dead.

Scene 16.

JOHN: Then what happened?

VOICE ONE: She had to go back to the States.

JOHN: She's probably waiting for your call.

VOICE ONE: You think so?

JOHN: I know so. Do you love her?

VOICE ONE: I think so. Back to work.

JOHN: Let's talk some more about—

VOICE ONE: Later. Why cottaging?

JOHN: Why do you go to the pubs every night?

VOICE ONE: That's not the same thing.

JOHN: It is.

VOICE ONE: Let's start again. Why cottaging?

JOHN: I don't know.

VOICE ONE: Do you find it exciting—having sex in toilets?

JOHN: No. Yes, but that's not the reason I—

VOICE ONE: You have difficulty meeting men for sex.

JOHN: No, not really.

VOICE ONE: Difficulty in meeting men?

JOHN: Yes.

VOICE ONE: What about the clubs? Don't you go—

JOHN: Sure, I go. Sometimes. And sometimes I wonder why I even bother.

VOICE ONE: Why?

JOHN: Because everyone there looks intimidating, dressed to the nines. Most of them talk among themselves, have a good time, laughing and drinking with their perfect smiles and perfect hair. And I spend the whole night standing alone in a dark corner. Pretending I'm having a barrel of laughs, pretending I'm having a good time. Pretending I'm enjoying the music. Tapping my feet and nodding my head to the rhythm. And waiting for someone to say something to me. Something nice. Say anything to me. Perhaps it's just that I'm Oriental.

VOICE ONE: Why do you say that?

JOHN: White guys aren't into Orientals.

VOICE ONE: There must be some.

JOHN: Some. Old ones maybe. Looking for a houseboy. Trying to relive the old colonial days. Or they are just fascinated by our culture. Like you. I know I'm not being fair, but that's the way I feel. Sometimes I wish I was— (*He laughs.*)

VOICE ONE: What's so funny?

JOHN: Nothing.

VOICE ONE: Tell me.

JOHN: I wanted to say—sometimes I wish I was—

VOICE ONE: What?

JOHN: White.

VOICE ONE: Why?

JOHN: I don't know. I see pictures of handsome, white guys hugging, kissing, holding hands in magazines like they were meant
for each other. Always white guys. But always happy. Always
together. Even in pornography. I see good-looking white guys
fucking each other, making love to each other. I don't know. I
see myself in those pictures, those magazines, videos. Suddenly
I'm that beautiful white guy everybody wants to make love to.
I don't know. Maybe it's just I've always found it difficult to—

VOICE ONE: Blend in?

JOHN: No. To belong.

VOICE ONE: What would you like to say to those people in the gay
clubs?

JOHN: Nothing.

VOICE ONE: There must be something. Let's pretend I'm one of
those people in the clubs.

JOHN: This is stupid.

VOICE ONE: It's not. Come on.

JOHN: I don't know what to say.

VOICE ONE: Say whatever's on your mind. Tell me how you feel. I
am one of those people you see in a club every weekend. I am
standing here with my friends.

JOHN: I can't.

VOICE ONE: Try, John. Tell me how and what you've been feeling.

JOHN: I don't know what to say.

VOICE ONE: Try saying hello.

JOHN: Hi.

VOICE ONE: Hi. (*Pause.*) Yes?

JOHN: I want—to let you know—that I wish you were a little more receptive, more hospitable, welcoming—

VOICE ONE: Carry on.

JOHN: It's not too much to ask, is it? After all, aren't we the same? Can you perhaps smile in my direction? Perhaps speak to me.

VOICE ONE: And?

JOHN: We—we don't have to sleep together. We don't have to—fuck. Maybe we can be friends. Maybe we can dance a little. Maybe see a movie, have dinner together. Maybe laugh a little. Maybe something. I can't anymore, let's stop this.

VOICE ONE: That's good.

JOHN: What's good? I may think all these thoughts, but then I'm back where I started. I find myself standing in that dark corner again. People passing me by. Not smiling. Not saying a word. And I go home alone. It's not so bad going home alone—except sometimes I wish—

VOICE ONE: Yes.

JOHN: To be honest with you, I hate the toilets. I really do—but there's this trembling in me when I'm there—I don't know what it is, but I like it—I enjoy it. And—and there's people there who want me. Even for a moment. And the idiot that I am—thinking I really belong—thinking perhaps all these moments will amount to something—someone who will—like me, love me— Isn't that the silliest thing you've heard?

VOICE ONE: No.

JOHN: It's sick.

VOICE ONE: No.

JOHN: I just want to be held by these men. For a moment, they do. Hold me. And almost all the time, I treasure that moment. The moment they smile. Then I go back and take a long, hot shower. Washing off every memory, every touch, and every smell. Only it never quite leaves me. No matter how hard or how long I wash. The dirt, filth penetrates deep into your skin. And for a time I'd try to stay away from the toilet, until that familiar loneliness—the need to be held. It's strange. This feeling. This marriage of dirt and desire. The beauty and the beast. It's pathetic. Sometimes I hate myself.

(JOHN *crushes a paper crane.*)

Scene 17.

VOICE ONE: The door of the toilet stall.

VOICE FOUR: Open.

VOICE TWO: John is leaning.

VOICE THREE: Against the wall.

VOICE ONE: Looking spent.

VOICE FOUR: Eyes shut.

VOICE TWO: Tight.

VOICE THREE: A young man.

VOICE ONE: Kneeling on the floor.

VOICE FOUR: Gets up.

VOICE TWO: Pulls up his jeans.

VOICE THREE: Zips himself up.

VOICE ONE: Buckles his belt.

VOICE FOUR: The young man.

VOICE TWO: Throws a ball of toilet paper.

VOICE THREE: Into the bowl.

VOICE ONE: Spits twice.

VOICE FOUR: Gently pats John.

VOICE TWO: On the butt.

VOICE THREE: Walks quickly away from the stall.

VOICE ONE: Quickly, as if he has something to hide.

VOICE FOUR: John watches him leave.

VOICE TWO: Sits down.

VOICE THREE: Closes the door.

VOICE ONE: He looks up.

VOICE FOUR: At the toilet ceiling.

VOICE TWO: Paint peeling.

VOICE THREE: Interesting shapes.

VOICE ONE: Patterns.

VOICE FOUR: Like the clouds in the sky.

VOICE TWO: Like the blot test cards.

VOICE THREE: It can be anything you want it to be.

VOICE ONE: Depending on how you see it.

VOICE FOUR: And where.

VOICE TWO: In the meanwhile, John sits.

VOICE THREE: Waiting.

VOICE ONE: Waiting.

VOICE FOUR: Waiting.

VOICE TWO: And waiting.

Scene 18.

VOICE THREE: Tell me, officer, in what capacity were you involved with the recent arrest in the toilets at Holland Park?

VOICE TWO: I arrested a suspect who was exposing himself to me.

VOICE THREE: Can you be more specific, please?

VOICE TWO: I was using the public convenience in Holland Park a few weeks ago.

VOICE THREE: Were you in uniform?

VOICE TWO: No.

VOICE THREE: Why?

VOICE TWO: I was off duty.

VOICE THREE: Really?

VOICE TWO: Yes.

VOICE THREE: Undercover?

VOICE TWO: Uh—no.

VOICE THREE: Go on.

VOICE TWO: A man in his thirties beckoned to me.

VOICE THREE: What do you mean "beckoned"? Did he call you? Whisper to you? Signaled?

VOICE TWO: He nodded to me.

VOICE THREE: You've never seen this man before?

VOICE TWO: No.

VOICE THREE: I see. Please go on.

VOICE TWO: As I said, the gentleman beckoned to me. Saying he had something to show me. He went into the toilet stall, and I followed. Then he unzipped his trousers and started to play with— I arrested him for public indecency.

VOICE THREE: Let me see. He beckoned to you. Nodded, I mean.

VOICE TWO: Yes.

VOICE THREE: He said he had something—

VOICE TWO: Something to show me. Yes.

VOICE THREE: You actually believed that he had something to—

VOICE TWO: Yes. I was curious.

VOICE THREE: I see, curious. And you followed him.

VOICE TWO: Yes.

VOICE THREE: Into the cubicle.

VOICE TWO: Yes.

VOICE THREE: Alone.

VOICE TWO: Yes.

VOICE THREE: And he took off his trousers.

VOICE TWO: Yes.

VOICE THREE: And you were standing there—still watching him.

VOICE TWO: That's right.

VOICE THREE: Then he started to fondle himself—and you were still standing there watching.

VOICE TWO: Yes.

VOICE THREE: And after a while, you arrested him.

VOICE TWO: Yes.

VOICE THREE: How long was this? Fifteen minutes? Ten minutes? Half an hour?

VOICE TWO: A minute. Thereabouts.

VOICE THREE: That long.

VOICE TWO: I had to be sure—

VOICE THREE: Sure that he was actually fondling his penis?

VOICE TWO: Right.

VOICE THREE: Stroking it?

VOICE TWO: Yes.

VOICE THREE: Sounds like police entrapment.

VOICE TWO: Does it? It wasn't.

VOICE THREE: Thank you. I'll take your word for it.

Scene 19.

VOICE ONE: Then what happened?

JOHN: After we did what we did in the toilet, I thought Will was going to leave—you know, like the others—without a word—just walk away—but then—he asked me if I wanted to have a drink with him in a nearby pub.

VOICE FOUR: I don't know why I asked him after we got off at the loo. Listen, this isn't what I usually do. Make friends at the public loos. Guess I was thirsty and since there wasn't anyone else around in the loo that evening. And I had no plans. I thought after a few drinks at the corner pub I could ask him back to my place so that we could get off again. (*To* JOHN.) Hiya.

JOHN: Hi.

VOICE FOUR: What's your name?

JOHN: John.

VOICE FOUR: Will. Say, do you fancy a drink?

JOHN: Sure. Yes. (*A beat.*) Of course I went. I mean there was this guy who I wanted—fancied very much and he's asking me out. He had a lager and I had a Coke. We talked about what music we liked.

VOICE FOUR: Opera. Puccini.

JOHN: Pet Shop Boys.

VOICE FOUR: Oh.

JOHN: Books.

VOICE FOUR: Bronte.

JOHN: All of them?

VOICE FOUR: Yes.

JOHN: I don't read much, except for schoolbooks.

VOICE FOUR: Hmm.

JOHN: What do you do?

VOICE FOUR: I'm a builder.

JOHN: Really?

VOICE FOUR: Uh-huh.

JOHN: I'm going to Cambridge in a few months. But right now I'm working in a big furniture shop at Whitelands. You know it? They've got nice things. A bit pricey for me, I'm afraid. I'd love to be able to shop there one day, instead of just—oh, I used to work at my father's restaurant—as a waiter. Didn't like it, so I got this job at—

VOICE FOUR: Really.

JOHN: I've been rambling—

VOICE FOUR: No.

JOHN: Uh-huh.

VOICE FOUR: It's getting late.

JOHN: Yes.

VOICE FOUR: Listen, do you want to come over? To my flat?

JOHN: Sure.

VOICE FOUR: Good.

JOHN: And I spent the night there.

VOICE ONE: How did you feel?

JOHN: High like a kite. Like the whole world was under my feet. Like nothing could go wrong. Nothing. I couldn't believe this was happening. To me, especially. We made love again and again. It was tender and urgent. That night was very special for me. Later in bed we talked a little more about what we liked, what we didn't. Less awkwardly than we did in the pub. He put on some music, hummed to it around the small flat and made some coffee. Then he talked about football. Suddenly his eyes lit up with a fiery green intensity. Going on about the F.A. Cup, which teams were his favorite and which teams were bound to make it to the finals. Don't know why. Don't know why all of a sudden I liked football. I never did before.

VOICE ONE: So William was very special to you then?

JOHN: I suppose so.

VOICE ONE: Then why did it happen?

JOHN: It just did.

Scene 20.

VOICE TWO: The crow flew across the field.

VOICE THREE: To the tree where the sparrows lived.

VOICE ONE: At first the sparrows looked at the crow.

VOICE FOUR: Some with suspicion and curiosity.

VOICE TWO: The others with fear, contempt, and hatred.

VOICE THREE: Time went by.

VOICE ONE: The crow couldn't be happier.

VOICE FOUR: It often flew with the sparrows.

VOICE TWO: Braving new heights.

VOICE THREE: A soul lost in love.

VOICE ONE: For the very first time, the crow felt free.

VOICE FOUR: Happy.

VOICE TWO: However, the crow flew haphazardly.

VOICE THREE: Ungracefully.

VOICE ONE: Clumsily.

VOICE FOUR: Often colliding with the other sparrows.

VOICE TWO: The sparrows were far too genteel.

VOICE THREE: Polite.

VOICE ONE: Embarrassed to say anything.

VOICE FOUR: Refused to confront the crow about its eating habits.

VOICE TWO: Slurping slimy worms in a vulgar fashion.

VOICE THREE: Eating voraciously.

VOICE ONE: Gorging greedily.

VOICE FOUR: Eating much more than the petite appetites the sparrows possessed.

VOICE TWO: Another topic of private discussion.

VOICE THREE: The crow's enthusiastic singing.

VOICE ONE: The sparrows chirped ever so heavenly.

VOICE FOUR: Mellifluously.

VOICE TWO: Superfluously.

VOICE THREE: The crow cawed hysterically.

VOICE ONE: An unbearable pitch.

VOICE FOUR: Out of tune.

VOICE TWO: Out of rhythm.

VOICE THREE: Loudly.

VOICE ONE: The sparrows winced painfully.

VOICE FOUR: Turned a deaf ear.

VOICE TWO: Smiled forcefully.

VOICE THREE: In time the sparrows accepted the crow.

VOICE ONE: Despite the way it ate.

VOICE FOUR: Flew.

VOICE TWO: And sang.

VOICE THREE: A part of their family.

VOICE ONE: The crow was happy.

Scene 21.

VOICE FOUR: Do you want to hear some music?

JOHN: Sure.

VOICE FOUR: What do you want to hear?

JOHN: Anything.

(VOICE FOUR *mimes putting on a CD.*)

JOHN: What's that?

VOICE FOUR: *Madame Butterfly.* It's my favorite.

JOHN: It's nice.

VOICE FOUR: Beautiful.

JOHN: What are they saying?

VOICE FOUR: "I'm happy now, so happy. Love me with a little love, a childlike love."

JOHN: Will, did you know it's been two weeks since we first met?

VOICE FOUR: Really?

JOHN: Yes. Can you believe it?

VOICE FOUR: What time is it?

JOHN: About eleven-thirty.

VOICE FOUR: I have to get up early tomorrow.

JOHN: Me too.

VOICE FOUR: I'm dead tired.

JOHN: I should go soon.

VOICE FOUR: Lie beside me.

JOHN: Hmm, I can hear your heart beating.

VOICE FOUR: You feel nice and smooth.

(They kiss tenderly.)

JOHN: You know something?

VOICE FOUR: What?

JOHN: I'm happy.

VOICE FOUR: Good.

JOHN: Really happy.

VOICE FOUR: Good.

JOHN: Will, we should go out the next time.

VOICE FOUR: The pictures?

JOHN: No.

VOICE FOUR: You mean to the pubs?

JOHN: Yeah, we always seem to stay in—not that I mind, of course.

VOICE FOUR: I'm not comfortable with those types of people.

JOHN: What do you mean?

VOICE FOUR: Well, I don't want to risk being recognized by anyone I know in those places.

JOHN: Sure, okay, I understand. Going to the pubs isn't that important, anyway. Besides I like being here. Being with you.

Scene 22.

VOICE TWO: Public sex has always been a part of the gay culture. Parks and health club saunas and shower rooms and YMCAs.

VOICE THREE: Isn't it illegal in the U.K.?

VOICE TWO: Yes.

VOICE THREE: Why sex in public places?

VOICE TWO: I'm not sure I'm qualified to answer why gay people are involved in such activities.

VOICE THREE: Do you think cottaging is a kind of perversion?

VOICE TWO: No, I don't think it's a perversion. Perhaps a better word is "choice." After all, it's among consenting adults. The cause of cottaging is directly related to the society's discrimination of homosexuals. Instead of providing a healthy and acceptable environment for gay men to come out to the public, they are often forced to meet other gay men in less than conventional surroundings.

VOICE THREE: So you're saying that toilet sex is the fault of the society?

VOICE TWO: No, I'm trying to say that it is the result of public inacceptance and intolerance of gays that has led them to seek—

VOICE THREE: You have your clubs and pubs.

VOICE TWO: We also have job discrimination, police harassment, gay bashings, poor AIDS health care—

VOICE THREE: What about AIDS? Don't you think—

VOICE TWO: AIDS should be a paramount concern for all those who have sex in public places.

VOICE THREE: Do you think toilet sex spreads homosexuality?

VOICE TWO: One does not spread homosexuality, and besides not only gay men are involved but bisexual and straight men like yourself as well.

VOICE THREE: That doesn't answer—

VOICE TWO: If you'd excuse me, I feel that this interview must come to an end. Does the word *homophobia* mean anything to you?

Scene 23.

VOICE ONE: Has Will treated you unkindly at all?

JOHN: No.

VOICE ONE: Not once?

JOHN: No.

VOICE ONE: Every couple must have their ups and downs.

JOHN: We had our differences.

VOICE ONE: What differences?

JOHN: Will could be—excitable.

VOICE ONE: Excitable?

JOHN: Aggressive.

VOICE ONE: Did you mind?

JOHN: I suppose not in the beginning, but later it started to—

VOICE ONE: To what?

JOHN: To hurt.

VOICE ONE: Uh-huh.

JOHN: He cared for me. I know he did. In his own way. There were times after we made love, he'd stroke my head, breathing softly. Soft brown hair. And skin like porcelain. Smooth. White. Pure. But there were times—

(VOICE ONE *reaches for his lighter and cigarettes and is about to smoke.*)

JOHN: You know, Jack, smoking isn't good for you. Cancer.

VOICE ONE: Yeah, I know.

JOHN: Hope I'm not being too—

VOICE ONE: You're not. Thanks.

JOHN: Sure. By the way, what's her name?

VOICE ONE: Whose name?

JOHN: The woman you were seeing.

VOICE ONE: Eh—Sue—Suzanne.

JOHN: Did you ring her?

VOICE ONE: Yes.

JOHN: And?

VOICE ONE: We're going to work it out.

JOHN: You know, we were happy. Will and I. Really happy together.

Scene 24.

The stage is pitch black. VOICE FOUR *is drunk and is walking heavily on stage.*

VOICE FOUR: Can't see a fucking thing in here.

JOHN: Do you want me to turn on the lights?

VOICE FOUR: No, no.

JOHN: Said you'd be here at eight. It's twelve now.

VOICE FOUR: Nag, nag, nag. Put on some music.

JOHN: What do you want to hear?

VOICE FOUR: Whatever's on the turntable.

JOHN: Not *Madame Butterfly* again.

VOICE FOUR: I like it.

JOHN: We always hear it.

VOICE FOUR: I thought you liked it.

JOHN: I did.

VOICE FOUR: Then put on something you like.

JOHN: What's this?

VOICE FOUR: *Carmen.* (VOICE FOUR *hums to the music. Sounds of* VOICE FOUR *knocking against furniture.*)

VOICE FOUR: Fuck. Where are you?

JOHN: Here.

VOICE FOUR: Where's here?

JOHN: By the bed.

VOICE FOUR: How convenient.

JOHN: I'm not in the mood.

VOICE FOUR: You will be.

JOHN: Ouch. Stop it. You're hurting me.

VOICE FOUR: You like it.

JOHN: I don't. (*Pause.*) Ouch. Will!

VOICE FOUR: Come here.

JOHN: You're late.

VOICE FOUR: So?

JOHN: You kept me waiting for hours.

VOICE FOUR: It's only a few hours.

JOHN: Where were you?

VOICE FOUR: At the pub.

JOHN: Again?

VOICE FOUR: Why are you so possessive?

JOHN: You kept me waiting.

VOICE FOUR: You had the bloody telly.

JOHN: I came over to see you, not watch telly.

VOICE FOUR: Come here and touch it.

JOHN: Stop it.

VOICE FOUR: You want it. Come on.

JOHN: No.

VOICE FOUR: I'm horny.

JOHN: You're drunk.

VOICE FOUR: I'm not.

JOHN: You smell of lager.

VOICE FOUR: You smell of talcum.

JOHN: I hate it when you're like that.

VOICE FOUR: I'm hard.

JOHN: Get off me now!

VOICE FOUR: You want it.

(*Sound of* JOHN's *chair falling on the floor, followed by sounds of a violent struggle.*)

JOHN: You're hurting me.

VOICE FOUR: You like that.

JOHN: I don't.

VOICE FOUR: Suck it.

JOHN: No.

VOICE FOUR: Suck it.

JOHN: Fuck you.

(*Sound of a slap.*)

JOHN (*whimpering*): That hurts.

VOICE FOUR: That'll teach you, you fucking tease.

(*Sound of a struggle.*)

JOHN: Will, stop it. Stop it.

VOICE FOUR: Suck this.

(*Sound of gagging.*)

VOICE FOUR: You like it, don't you? Come on, tell me you like it.

(JOHN *responds inaudibly, still gagging.*)

VOICE FOUR: That's it. Take it all in, you cocksucker.

(JOHN *again responds gaggingly and in deep breaths.*)

VOICE FOUR: Yeah, yeah. That's good. Lick my balls. Lick it. Now, suck it. Hard. Yeah. (*He breathes hard.*) Stop. I don't want to come yet. Turn over. I want to fuck you.

JOHN: No.

(*Sound of a vicious slap.*)

VOICE FOUR: Shut the fuck up.

JOHN: Will.

(*Another slap.*)

VOICE FOUR: You want it. My big cock up your arse.

JOHN: Condom.

VOICE FOUR: Fuck condoms.

JOHN: You promised you'd use—

VOICE FOUR: Shut up.

JOHN: Condoms.

(*Suddenly* JOHN *screams in agony.*)

VOICE FOUR: Yes. Nice and tight, the way I like it.

JOHN (*moaning*): Will. Take it out. Now.

VOICE FOUR: It feels good.

JOHN: Will. Condom. Please.

VOICE FOUR: Tight.

JOHN: Put it on.

VOICE FOUR: Yes.

JOHN: Will.

VOICE FOUR: You like my tongue in your ear?

JOHN: Don't. (*Pause.*) Mmm.

VOICE FOUR: Feels good.

JOHN: Yes.

VOICE FOUR: Do I feel good?

JOHN: You feel good.

VOICE FOUR: Do you like it?

JOHN: Yes.

VOICE FOUR: You wanted it, didn't you?

JOHN: Yes.

VOICE FOUR: Tell me you want it.

JOHN: I want it. Yes.

VOICE FOUR: Say it again.

JOHN: I want it.

VOICE FOUR: I can't hear you.

JOHN: I want it!

VOICE FOUR: Louder.

JOHN (*loudly*): I want it!

VOICE FOUR: Want what?

JOHN: You! I want you! I want you! I want you! I love you.

VOICE FOUR: I'm coming!

(VOICE FOUR *groans. Both he and* JOHN *breathe hard and slow. Then silence.*)

Scene 25.

VOICE TWO: They cannot see? See me?

VOICE THREE: No. You'll be in silhouette.

VOICE TWO: See-lo—what?

VOICE THREE: You'll be in shadows.

VOICE TWO: I'm in shadows. Okay. Shadows.

VOICE THREE: And the money will be—

VOICE TWO: Don't want to talk. About money now. Not now.

VOICE THREE: Tell me about John. John Lee. Your son.

(Pause.)

VOICE TWO: I have only one son. Lone. I don't know why he change his name to John—English. Maybe he want to be like English friends in school—not be different. Be like them. I remember one day—when he was in primary school—he come home from school—clothes all dirty—got mud all over—school tie torn—books in schoolbag all tear up—small pieces—his hands, legs, nose all got blood—but he never say one word. Nothing. But this is life. Life here. Have to accept. Have to learn. Even change name cannot do anything. He don't like much Chinese way of life. Always question the way Chinese live, Chinese speak. He once criticize way I speak English—I angry, hit him across face till red. Again he never say one word. Give him work here at restaurant. Don't want to work here. Say don't understand people speaking Chinese, so how can take order? He find another job in furniture shop. Deep inside, I know he hate working here. Remind him too much of who he is. Where he came from. I come from Singapore long time—in sixties—sacrifice everything I have so children can have good life in England. Think children will be able to be better than other children in Singapore. But think I make mistake. Big mistake. I have daughter who shame my family. Go about with a lot of white men. Stay at their house at night. I know. I know. Times not the same. Different. Have to accept. Now I have son who no respect me. But he intelligent and go to university very soon. Now no more university. No more son. Neighbor all talk behind my back—of murder. In toilet. Bethnal Green. I so ashamed. So angry. Every morning open restaurant in Gerard Street selling noodle bowls, rice plates. People polite, but I know their minds, their hearts. I see it in eyes. Those silent eyes very loud. My wife pretend nothing happen. Pretend everything okay. Everyone all pretending around me. All pretending. My son no commit crime. No commit murder. My son no homo. No homo! He cannot be—I—I have no son. Son is dead. Dead to me. Dead. Perhaps better he change his name to English. Be someone else.

Scene 26.

JOHN: You look like shit.

VOICE ONE: Late night.

JOHN: Again?

VOICE ONE: I'm predictable.

JOHN: Why do you do that so often?

VOICE ONE: Do what often?

JOHN: Go out to the pubs and drink.

VOICE ONE: Because I can't think of anything better to do.

JOHN: Really?

VOICE ONE: I need to—

JOHN: Get laid.

VOICE ONE: Let's get back to the session. Tell me what happened
that afternoon at Bethnal Green.

JOHN: Nothing.

VOICE ONE: Stop fucking about! I thought we had an honest relationship.

JOHN: We do.

VOICE ONE: Then?

JOHN: I don't want to talk about it.

VOICE ONE: You'll have to. Sooner or later.

JOHN: I don't.

VOICE ONE: Listen, you've got to bloody confront it once and for all.

JOHN: You're only here to finish a report.

VOICE ONE: Yes. But I'm also here to help—

JOHN: I don't want your help, I've told you.

VOICE ONE: You need my help.

JOHN: No, I don't.

VOICE ONE: Well, fuck you! Yes. Fuck you. Fuck all of this.

JOHN: You'll never understand. You can't—

VOICE ONE: How do you know I won't understand if you don't tell me the story. We've been playing this pissy, merry-go-round question-and-answer session all week and I've gotten nowhere. I want to fucking know what happened.

JOHN: No.

VOICE ONE: You're always so fucking high and mighty about how people don't understand where you're coming from. So you're Oriental—a Chink. So you're gay, poof, queer. So what? Now's your chance to tell me. To make me understand why you fucking did what you did.

JOHN: You'll never understand.

VOICE ONE: Maybe not. But tell me.

JOHN: No.

VOICE ONE: Come on, John. Try. Trust me.

(VOICE ONE *puts his hand on* JOHN's *shoulder*.)

JOHN: I don't know where to begin.

VOICE ONE: Where did you get the gun?

JOHN: It belonged to my father. Kept it in the restaurant. Just in case of robbers, he said. Said everyone had one, why shouldn't he? Don't know where he got the gun from. It's illegal, probably, just like Pa to do something like that. I took the gun from him.

VOICE ONE: Why?

JOHN: Maybe I just wanted to. Take the gun.

VOICE ONE: To shoot someone?

JOHN: Maybe.

VOICE ONE: William Hope?

JOHN: Maybe.

VOICE ONE: Why?

JOHN: Because.

VOICE ONE: Because?

JOHN: Because. (*Pause.*) He didn't speak to me for several days—days turned into weeks—I don't know—I tried ringing him—leaving messages—on his answering machine, but he didn't ring back. So that Saturday afternoon, I decided to go over to his flat. I wanted to see him. Just to talk or something. But when I arrived at his place, I didn't ring the doorbell. Didn't even use the latch key he gave me. All I did was to stand outside a bus stop across the street. Looking at his flat with the gun in my jacket.

VOICE THREE: And what happened after that, John?

JOHN: Two–three hours later, he stepped outside. Will did. Probably taking a walk. I followed him. And all the time I was following him, I had an uncomfortable but certain feeling I knew where he was going.

VOICE THREE: To the lav in Bethnal Green.

JOHN: I said maybe not.

VOICE TWO: Maybe he's going to the tube station.

JOHN: Shopping.

VOICE THREE: Maybe a walk in the park.

JOHN: Maybe.

VOICE TWO: Maybe some groceries at Sainsbury's.

JOHN: Maybe a drink at the pub.

VOICE THREE: Maybe he's meeting some friends.

JOHN: What friends?

VOICE TWO: And?

JOHN: And he walked into the lav.

VOICE THREE: I was crushed.

VOICE TWO: Destroyed.

VOICE THREE: But I knew it.

JOHN: Maybe that's why I followed him.

VOICE TWO: To confirm my suspicions.

VOICE THREE: Maybe that's why I took the gun.

JOHN: Maybe.

VOICE TWO: The cheating bastard.

JOHN: I stopped outside. Didn't want to go in. Didn't dare.

VOICE THREE: Dare what?

JOHN: Dare to confront him.

VOICE TWO: Dare to hear the truth?

VOICE THREE: See the truth?

VOICE TWO: Dare to use the gun?

JOHN: I don't know.

VOICE THREE: Maybe he's really taking a piss.

VOICE TWO: Maybe.

VOICE THREE: Yeah. Right.

JOHN: I don't know. Then I saw people, men, going into the lav. But no one came out. For the longest time. I kept fingering my gun.

VOICE TWO: That son of a bitch.

VOICE THREE: You are an idiot.

VOICE TWO: I knew it.

VOICE THREE: All the time.

VOICE TWO: Why? Why are you doing this?

VOICE THREE: Kill him.

JOHN: Feeling the cold steel in my pocket. I start‹
tal notes of who went in and who went out.

VOICE TWO: Young black guy with an Adidas sports bag.

VOICE FOUR: White guy in his thirties carrying the *Independent*.

VOICE THREE: Old man in a brown blazer.

VOICE FOUR: White boy with a baseball cap.

VOICE TWO: Still he didn't come out.

JOHN: Then when I thought no one was in there anymore, I walked
into the lav.

VOICE THREE: The gun.

VOICE TWO: The loo was empty.

VOICE THREE: Deathly quiet.

VOICE TWO: Deathly still.

VOICE THREE: The gun pressed against his jacket.

VOICE TWO: Pressed against his beating heart.

JOHN: Then I saw Will in the cubicle. Pretending to take a piss.

VOICE THREE: He was pulling his cock.

VOICE TWO: Deliberately.

JOHN: He seemed surprised to see me.

VOICE THREE: Almost frightened.

ᴠɪᴄᴇ ᴛᴡᴏ: Shocked.

ᴊᴏʜɴ: Hi.

ᴠᴏɪᴄᴇ ꜰᴏᴜʀ: Hi. Fancy bumping into you, here of all places.

ᴊᴏʜɴ: Yes. Fancy that.

ᴠᴏɪᴄᴇ ᴛʜʀᴇᴇ: Awkward silence.

ᴠᴏɪᴄᴇ ᴛᴡᴏ: The gun.

ᴠᴏɪᴄᴇ ᴛʜʀᴇᴇ: Outside traffic noises.

ᴠᴏɪᴄᴇ ꜰᴏᴜʀ: Eh—everyone's gone.

ᴊᴏʜɴ: Really.

ᴠᴏɪᴄᴇ ꜰᴏᴜʀ: So how have you been?

ᴊᴏʜɴ: Good.

ᴠᴏɪᴄᴇ ꜰᴏᴜʀ: You all right? You look kinda—

ᴊᴏʜɴ: You didn't call.

ᴠᴏɪᴄᴇ ꜰᴏᴜʀ: I was busy. Work, you know.

ᴊᴏʜɴ: I rang. Left messages.

ᴠᴏɪᴄᴇ ꜰᴏᴜʀ: I know.

ᴊᴏʜɴ: You could have called.

ᴠᴏɪᴄᴇ ꜰᴏᴜʀ: I know, but I was busy—

ᴊᴏʜɴ: I must have left you a thousand messages.

ᴠᴏɪᴄᴇ ꜰᴏᴜʀ: Yeah.

ᴊᴏʜɴ: I didn't hear from you at all.

VOICE FOUR: Listen, do you want to go outside so we can talk?

JOHN: No. Let's talk here. It's quieter.

VOICE FOUR: Outside.

JOHN: Here. I want to talk—

VOICE FOUR: All right, here. (*Pause.*) Well?

JOHN: You look—

VOICE TWO: John reached out to touch his face.

VOICE FOUR: I'm okay. Really.

VOICE THREE: Brushing me away.

VOICE TWO: The gun.

VOICE THREE: Against my heart.

JOHN: I—

VOICE TWO: Helpless.

VOICE THREE: Awkward.

VOICE TWO: Stupid.

VOICE FOUR: Look, sorry I didn't ring back.

JOHN: You said you were busy.

VOICE FOUR: I wasn't busy.

JOHN: I see. It's okay.

VOICE FOUR: No, it's not.

JOHN: It is. Really.

VOICE FOUR: Don't think you understand. Johnny, I like you—I really do—but—I think—

JOHN: We should stop seeing each other.

VOICE FOUR: Yes.

JOHN: Why?

VOICE FOUR: Don't like this situation, that's all.

JOHN: What situation?

VOICE FOUR: Us. Us meeting. Us doing things together.

JOHN: Us fucking each other.

VOICE FOUR: Yes.

JOHN: Why?

VOICE FOUR: Don't know why. I just don't want it.

JOHN: Then why are you here? (*Pause.*) I'm sorry.

VOICE FOUR: That's not the point.

JOHN: Forget it.

VOICE FOUR: Let me get to the point. It's over, okay?

JOHN: He said it very evenly—calm.

VOICE FOUR: We are history. Okay? I'm not what you think I am. I'm not that way. I enjoyed doing what we do. But I'm not—queer.

JOHN: Like me.

VOICE FOUR: Told you from the start that I date women, and I like to fool around with guys—you know just to get off—but I'm not like that—like you. And I don't want to play games, the idea of hiding every time—hide and seek. People may start getting strange ideas about me and you—might start thinking we're queer—that I'm queer—something I'm not. Don't misunderstand, whatever we had—was great. I enjoyed it—had a great time—I know you did too—I don't know, but maybe I just didn't like the idea of turning—perhaps we could be friends.

JOHN: But I wasn't listening. Not a word. All I heard was—

VOICE FOUR: It's over.

VOICE TWO: It's over.

VOICE THREE: It's over.

JOHN: Like some strange, hypnotic melody dancing in my mind.

VOICE TWO: Intoxicating me.

VOICE THREE: Suffocating me.

JOHN: Somehow I anticipated this. I knew this was going to happen.

VOICE TWO: Him leaving.

JOHN: Him saying just that.

VOICE THREE: But he doesn't know better.

JOHN: Maybe that's why I took the gun.

VOICE TWO: Maybe.

JOHN: Maybe I was expecting he'd say this.

VOICE THREE: Maybe.

JOHN: He belonged to me. Only to me.

VOICE TWO: And you took the gun.

JOHN: To make him stay.

VOICE THREE: Force him to stay.

JOHN: No matter what. I was pleading—pleading with him.

VOICE TWO: Begging.

JOHN: Raising my voice. Anything to make him stay.

VOICE THREE: Please don't—

JOHN: Don't say—

VOICE TWO: Please, I'm sorry—

JOHN: I won't anymore.

VOICE FOUR: Listen, this has nothing to—

JOHN: Will, please, you can't—

VOICE FOUR: I'm not queer, Johnny! I'm not one of your kind. I—I've got nothing against—you—your kind—at all. This whole thing was all in your head. Shouldn't have allowed it to happen the way it did—it went too far.

JOHN: I felt so helpless.

VOICE TWO: Desperate.

VOICE FOUR: It's over.

VOICE THREE: Angry.

VOICE TWO: Hurt.

VOICE FOUR: It's over.

VOICE THREE: Pained.

VOICE TWO: The gun.

VOICE THREE: In your jacket.

VOICE TWO: Waiting.

VOICE FOUR: Hey, Johnny, I'm sorry. Really am.

VOICE ONE: Final scene in Bizet's *Carmen.*

VOICE TWO: No.

JOHN: Don't go.

VOICE THREE: Not yet.

VOICE TWO: Please.

VOICE ONE: The Death Scene.

JOHN: Will smiled that smile, that familiar smile I always see in my mind whenever he's away from me.

VOICE THREE: He shrugged his shoulders.

VOICE ONE: Don José arrives at the bullring.

VOICE TWO: Will put his hands in his pockets.

VOICE THREE: And started to walk out of the toilet.

VOICE ONE: Don José begs for Carmen's love.

JOHN: I wanted to shout but no sound came out. No words.

VOICE TWO: You have a gun.

VOICE ONE: Carmen declares it's over between them.

VOICE THREE: You can make him stay.

VOICE TWO: Force him to stay.

VOICE ONE: Don José implores Carmen to return to him.

VOICE THREE: Then maybe he'll change his mind.

VOICE TWO: He'll see things your way.

VOICE ONE: A triumphant shout from the bullring!

VOICE THREE: Understand what you're trying to say.

VOICE TWO: What you feel.

VOICE ONE: The matador has plunged his sword into the bull.

VOICE THREE: Stay.

VOICE ONE: Plunge!

VOICE TWO: Stay.

VOICE ONE: Plunge!

VOICE THREE: Please stay.

VOICE ONE: Plunge!

VOICE TWO: Your gun.

VOICE ONE: Carmen admits the matador is her new lover.

JOHN: Then I remembered the gun.

VOICE THREE: Take it out.

VOICE TWO: Now!

VOICE ONE: The matador stabs the bull with his glistening blade.

JOHN: Took it out of my jacket.

VOICE ONE: Stab!

VOICE THREE: Aim.

VOICE ONE: Stab!

VOICE TWO: Shoot!

VOICE ONE: Stab!

VOICE THREE: He's walking away.

VOICE ONE: Don José realizes Carmen doesn't love him anymore.

VOICE THREE: He used you.

VOICE TWO: Like everyone else.

JOHN: I—I pointed it at his back.

VOICE THREE: I won't be used again.

VOICE TWO: Stay.

VOICE THREE: I want you.

VOICE TWO: Don't go.

VOICE ONE: Rage and despair overwhelms Don José.

VOICE THREE: Fuck you.

VOICE TWO: You're like the fucking rest.

VOICE THREE: A quick feel.

VOICE TWO: A willing mouth.

VOICE THREE: And a willing arse.

VOICE ONE: Don José pulls out his knife.

VOICE TWO: Love me.

VOICE THREE: Please stay.

JOHN: Stay!

VOICE ONE: The lusty knife glistening in the afternoon light.

VOICE FOUR: What the fuck?

VOICE TWO: Gun pointing to Will.

VOICE FOUR: You're bloody crazy.

VOICE ONE: The crowd cheers "Viva, viva!"

VOICE TWO: Queer!

VOICE ONE, TWO, and THREE: Viva! Viva!

VOICE THREE: Chink!

VOICE ONE, TWO, and THREE: Viva! Viva!

VOICE TWO: Poof!

VOICE ONE, TWO, and THREE: Viva! Viva!

VOICE THREE: Homo!

VOICE ONE, TWO, and THREE: Kill it!

JOHN: It is loaded.

VOICE THREE: Will looked at him.

VOICE TWO: In disbelief.

VOICE THREE: Snarled.

VOICE TWO: As if daring him to shoot.

VOICE ONE: Carmen laughs.

VOICE TWO: Will continued to go.

VOICE THREE: Stay.

VOICE TWO: What else can I do?

VOICE THREE: You're not walking out.

VOICE ONE: Don José raises the knife to his blood-red eyes.

JOHN: Will?

VOICE TWO: The gun trembled.

VOICE ONE: The matador thrusts his sword into the bull.

VOICE THREE: Don't go.

VOICE TWO: The gun swayed.

VOICE THREE: You're not going anywhere.

VOICE ONE: The bull collapses.

VOICE TWO: Under his sweaty fingers.

VOICE THREE: Stay!

VOICE ONE: The bullring is swimming in a sea of blood.

VOICE TWO: Wrapping around the trigger.

VOICE THREE: Stay!

VOICE ONE: The crowd is cheering and throwing roses.

VOICE TWO: Cock the pistol.

JOHN: Then I started to squeeze the trigger.

VOICE TWO: Bullet in the chamber.

VOICE THREE: Ready to fire.

JOHN: Will?

VOICE TWO: He continued walking.

VOICE ONE: Don José plunges the knife into Carmen.

JOHN: I love you.

VOICE THREE: Bang!

VOICE TWO: His body crumpled.

VOICE THREE: Like a paper crane against a flame.

VOICE TWO: And he fell against the white urinal.

VOICE THREE: His right hand clutching a side of the urinal.

VOICE TWO: Holding tight.

VOICE THREE: He was in shock.

VOICE TWO: You're not going.

JOHN: My hands were shaking.

VOICE TWO: Bang!

VOICE THREE: Another shot.

VOICE TWO: You're staying.

VOICE THREE: You need me!

VOICE TWO: You love me.

VOICE THREE: We'll be together.

VOICE ONE: Don José lifts the bloodstained knife.

VOICE TWO: We'll be happy.

VOICE THREE: Bang!

VOICE ONE: The knife plunges again!

JOHN: My eyes were closed tight. When I opened them, I found him on the floor.

VOICE TWO: Spread-eagled.

VOICE THREE: He was still moving.

VOICE TWO: Tough son of a bitch.

VOICE THREE: Gagging sounds.

VOICE TWO: Struggling towards the door of the toilet.

VOICE ONE: He was determined to walk out.

JOHN: Determined to leave me.

VOICE TWO: Motherfucker.

VOICE THREE: You cannot leave.

VOICE TWO: You'll stay.

VOICE ONE: Bang!

VOICE THREE: Bang!

VOICE TWO: Bang!

VOICE THREE: Six shots.

VOICE TWO: Then he was still.

VOICE ONE: No more cheering.

VOICE THREE: His body lay limp on the cold mosaic floor.

VOICE TWO: I've never seen so much red in my life.

VOICE THREE: Except when I was a child.

VOICE TWO: In Singapore.

VOICE THREE: Chinese New Year.

VOICE TWO: Red firecrackers littered the narrow streets.

VOICE THREE: Like withered leaves in autumn.

VOICE TWO: The whole toilet was red.

VOICE THREE: The white porcelain turned red.

JOHN (*softly and calmly*): Suddenly I felt drained of all energy and dropped the gun. I limped slowly toward his lifeless body and held him. Tight. Called him. Gently. Will? Will? But he didn't respond. Didn't move. His silent eyes looking at me. Like the way they used to. Hot tears suddenly filled my eyes. I started to rock him. Slowly like a baby. My baby. And then—I kissed him. On his still bloody lips. Lips turning cold. Oh god, what have I done? I didn't want to—didn't mean to—what have I done—what have I— (*Beat.*) I wanted to scream. Wanted to die.

I kept staring at the toilet. The pretty mosaic tiles—with patterns—flower patterns. Pretty flower patterns. They looked like they were dancing. Flower patterns covered with blood—all over the white tiles—and the walls—and the urinals—they were all red. Red. Red. Oh my god, I shot him. I shot him. I shot him.

(*An awkward silence. Suddenly* JOHN *screams at the top of his voice. It's an animal cry, a cry of anguish and pain that he has been harboring all this time. He screams repeatedly.*)

Scene 27.

VOICE TWO: The crow was happy.

VOICE FOUR: Content.

VOICE ONE: A part of this feathered family.

VOICE THREE: It sang merrily.

VOICE TWO: Ate and flew.

VOICE FOUR: Slept.

VOICE ONE: Played with the sparrows.

VOICE THREE: The days passed.

VOICE TWO: The crow felt homesick.

VOICE FOUR: It dawned upon the crow.

VOICE ONE: It will never truly belong with them.

VOICE THREE: The beautiful, chirpy, graceful, little sparrows.

VOICE TWO: The black crow may sing, eat, or fly with them.

VOICE FOUR: It will never feel like one of them.

VOICE ONE: Never be one of them.

VOICE THREE: A sparrow.

VOICE TWO: The crow was disheartened.

VOICE FOUR: Once again.

VOICE ONE: The crow bade its farewells.

VOICE THREE: Flew across the green field.

VOICE TWO: Back to the tree.

VOICE FOUR: Back to its family of crows.

VOICE ONE: Where it belonged.

VOICE THREE: Where it truly belonged.

VOICE TWO: Or so the crow thought.

VOICE FOUR: The other crows welcomed it back.

VOICE ONE: They flew and ate with their old friend.

VOICE THREE: Something wasn't quite the same.

VOICE TWO: The crow flew in fanciful circles.

VOICE FOUR: In the air, soaring up and down.

VOICE ONE: The crow ate little.

VOICE THREE: A genteel fashion.

VOICE TWO: The crow burst into song.

VOICE FOUR: Songs it had once sung in the company of sparrows.

VOICE ONE: The other crows found the crow distant.

VOICE THREE: Different.

VOICE TWO: Strange.

VOICE FOUR: Peculiar.

VOICE ONE: Queer.

VOICE THREE: They began avoiding the crow.

VOICE TWO: The crow was never more alone.

VOICE FOUR: It didn't belong to the sparrows or the crows.

VOICE ONE: Again the black crow packed its belongings.

VOICE THREE: It flew away.

VOICE TWO: From the tree of crows.

VOICE FOUR: From the tree of sparrows.

VOICE ONE: In search of another tree.

VOICE THREE: Another field.

VOICE TWO: Another family.

VOICE FOUR: Another life.

Scene 28.

VOICE ONE: How are you doing today?

JOHN: Fine.

VOICE ONE: That's good.

JOHN: You're through with the analysis, aren't you?

VOICE ONE: Yes. I'm going to submit my findings this—

JOHN: And you'll be too busy to come by.

VOICE ONE: Well, there isn't really a need for me to—

JOHN: I see.

VOICE ONE: But—I will. Once I finish the report.

JOHN: We can talk—

VOICE ONE: Sure.

JOHN: I'd like that very much.

(JOHN *reaches for* VOICE ONE's *hand and squeezes it.*)

VOICE ONE: Yeah.

JOHN: Good.

(VOICE ONE *squeezes* JOHN's *hand and pulls his hand away.*)

VOICE ONE: I'll come by. (*Pause.*) Has anyone come by to see you at all?

JOHN: No one.

VOICE ONE: Your parents?

JOHN: They're too embarrassed to come.

VOICE ONE: Sorry.

JOHN: I'm not. Are there any questions you have that I haven't answered?

VOICE ONE: No, not really.

JOHN: I don't mind. Any questions. Any at all. Perhaps I haven't been clear or—

VOICE ONE: None. None at all.

JOHN: I see. (*Pause.*) You know, he meant the world to me.

VOICE ONE: I know.

JOHN: I think you should put that down in your report.

VOICE ONE: I will.

JOHN: I had so many plans for the both of us.

VOICE ONE: Uh-huh.

JOHN: Dreams. Things we'd do together.

VOICE ONE: But he's gone now, John.

JOHN: Who's gone?

VOICE ONE: William Hope.

JOHN: Oh no, he's not.

VOICE ONE: What do you mean?

JOHN: He'll never be gone. Now I have him where I want him.

VOICE ONE: I don't understand.

JOHN: I've finally got Will all to myself now.

Scene 28.

VOICE THREE: Cigarette?

VOICE ONE: Eh—no, thank you. I've quit.

VOICE THREE: So you were saying, Suzanne, the woman you said you were romantically involved with, doesn't exist?

VOICE ONE: No, I invented her.

VOICE THREE: Why?

VOICE ONE: To gain someone's trust, you have to blemish the truth.

VOICE THREE: You told John Lee a personal story, and he told you his.

VOICE ONE: Old trade secret.

VOICE THREE: You lied to him.

VOICE ONE: I got what I wanted.

VOICE THREE: Isn't that unethical?

VOICE ONE: Isn't the basis of this whole interview?

VOICE THREE: So you found John Lee sane during the time of the murder?

VOICE ONE: Yes, I found him sane.

VOICE THREE: Why?

VOICE ONE: He was sane, like most of us. It was more of a crime of passion. He did truly love William Hope, but the relationship was not reciprocal.

VOICE THREE: Taking someone's life is a sane act?

VOICE ONE: No, but the circumstances surrounding the death were—You see, not all of us have the intense passion that John possessed—passion enough to kill the person he loved.

VOICE THREE: Aren't you making this case a little more romantic than you should?

VOICE ONE: Perhaps. But I think you'd probably find the same answers I did by going through the case.

VOICE THREE: This is certainly quite a change from what you told me before.

VOICE ONE: Yes, I know.

VOICE THREE: What was the verdict?

VOICE ONE: Life without parole.

VOICE THREE: Thank you, Dr. Worthing. We'll leave it there. Have you been back to see John Lee since the trial?

VOICE ONE: Eh—no. But I will. I did promise him I would—when my work's a little lighter. Listen, I've got to go.

VOICE THREE: One last question, Dr. Worthing. You never told me why he folded those paper cranes?

VOICE ONE: A Japanese tradition that if you folded the paper cranes—a thousand of them—your wish would come true.

VOICE THREE: And what wish did John Lee have? For folding the thousand paper cranes?

VOICE ONE: You mean you can't guess?

Scene 29.

VOICE FOUR: Bang.

VOICE TWO: Bang.

VOICE ONE: Bang.

VOICE THREE: Bang.

VOICE TWO: Bang.

VOICE FOUR: Bang.

VOICE TWO: Six shots.

VOICE THREE: A body falls.

VOICE FOUR: Hot blood splatters.

VOICE TWO: On the peeling walls.

VOICE THREE: On the cold, hard floor.

VOICE ONE: Red flower.

VOICE TWO: Patterns.

VOICE THREE: On white.

VOICE FOUR: Mosaic tiles.

VOICE TWO: On cool.

VOICE THREE: White porcelain.

VOICE ONE: Smells of.

VOICE FOUR: Gun smoke.

VOICE THREE: Antiseptic.

VOICE TWO: Urine.

VOICE THREE: Semen.

VOICE ONE: A boy.

VOICE FOUR: Holding a man.

VOICE THREE: Two of them.

VOICE FOUR: Alone.

VOICE TWO: In a public toilet.

VOICE ONE: At Bethnal Green.

VOICE TWO: Outside the tube station.

VOICE FOUR: Beside a small park.

VOICE THREE: With flowers.

VOICE ONE: And some trees.

VOICE FOUR: And in one particular tree.

VOICE TWO: A lone black crow.

VOICE ONE: Sits comfortably.

VOICE THREE: On a branch.

VOICE FOUR: Cawing.

VOICE THREE: Cawing.

VOICE ONE: Watching painfully.

VOICE TWO: Watching longingly.

VOICE ONE: The sparrows.

VOICE FOUR: In a nearby tree.

VOICE THREE: Singing.

VOICE FOUR: Sweetly.

VOICE TWO: Without a care in the world.

VOICE THREE: Bang!

VOICE ONE: Bang!

VOICE TWO: Bang!

VOICE FOUR: Bang!

VOICE ONE: Bang!

VOICE THREE: Bang!

VOICE TWO: Six shots.

JOHN: Two bodies fall.

(*Short pause and then gradually louder, the overlapping cacophony of London street sounds once again fills the air.*)

VOICE THREE: Tara, love. See you at four for tea. Don't forget the MacVities biscuits at the midnight shop. Chocolate ones, mind you—

VOICE ONE: Come on then, off to the pub. The F.A. Cup's about to start in a few minutes—

VOICE FOUR: Sorry, I can't come to the phone. Leave a message and I'll ring back. Bye—

VOICE TWO: Say, would you like to come in for a show? We've got topless girls—

VOICE THREE: Fucking terrorists. They've got the bleeding tubes all shut off because of a bomb scare. Now, how the fuck can I get to Camden?

VOICE FOUR: Do you want tickets to *Phantom*? I've got good seats for— Sorry, no speak Japanese. *Phantom*. Only one hundred quid for a ticket. Very little yen. Yes?—

VOICE ONE: Another crisis at Buckingham Palace. Now, next on the turntable is another member of the British royal family, Boy George—

VOICE THREE: (*Sound of cars honking.*)

VOICE TWO: (*Sound of an underground train leaving the platform.*)

VOICE FOUR: (*Sound of Big Ben striking four o'clock.*)

(JOHN *finishes folding a paper crane and looks at it incredulously. He holds it on the palm of his hand and offers it to the audience. He smiles.*)

End of Play.

A LANGUAGE
OF THEIR OWN

David Drake and B. D. Wong in the New York Shakespeare Festival's production of A Language of Their Own *(photograph by Michal Daniel)*

For John Palmerton

A Language of Their Own's original New York production, which opened on April 20, 1995, was presented by the New York Shakespeare Festival, George C. Wolfe, producer.

Oscar	Francis Jue
Ming	B. D. Wong
Daniel	Alec Mapa
Robert	David Drake

Director	Ong Keng Sen
Dramaturg	Shelby Jiggetts
Set Designer	Myunghee Cho
Lighting Designer	Scott Zielinski
Costume Designer	Michael Krass
Composer and Musician	Liang-Xing Tang
Fight Director	J. Steven White
Production Stage Manager	Buzz Cohen
Stage Manager	Rick Steiger

An earlier version of *A Language of Their Own* was presented in Los Angeles on May 6, 1994, by Celebration Theatre.

Oscar	Dennis Dun
Ming	Chris Tashima
Daniel	Noel Alumit
Robert	Anthony David

Director	Tim Dang
Dramaturg	Jason Jacobs
Set Designer	John Lee
Lighting Designer	Frank McKown
Stage Manager	Kevin Carroll

A Spartan set.

OSCAR, a thirtysomething Asian male, speaks English with a slight, unobtrusive accent. MING, a twentysomething Asian male, speaks American English.

In a series of monologues and dialogues, OSCAR and MING often speak to the audience, as if they were lawyers defending different points of view on the same case.

The playing and direction must never be obvious, sentimental, or heavy-handed. More is gained in subtext and subtlety, and by interpreting the darker tones of the characters and the play's themes.

The director may choose to employ a live musician in the production.

Learning Chinese

MING: I can never forget what he said to me.

OSCAR: I don't think we should see each other anymore.

MING: It wasn't unexpected. It had to happen the way things were going. Which was nowhere.

OSCAR: Of course, we can still be friends.

MING: Sure. Friends. If that's what you want.

OSCAR: That's not what I wanted. Not really. But it was all I could say. All I could do.

MING: Friends. A change of labels. From lovers to friends. It's the same person whom you have loved, made love to, thought about day in and day out. A person whose secrets, fears, and hopes were made known to you. Now that very same person is a friend. A person you have coffee with, a person you call when you want company to go to the theater, the movies, and the bars. Lovers to friends. Label musical chairs.

OSCAR: We can call each other up. Have coffee. Go to the movies or something.

MING: Or something. Yes. We'll be friends.

OSCAR: Good friends.

MING: Sure. Whatever.

OSCAR: You know, this is not easy to say.

MING: Please, get on with it.

OSCAR: It's not working out. We've become two very different people.

MING: You just don't become different people overnight.

OSCAR: What I'm trying to say is that things haven't been quite the same.

MING: Let's not start this—

OSCAR: Especially—

MING: You always—

OSCAR: Since the test.

MING: The test. You always bring it up.

OSCAR: It's the truth.

MING: It's not true.

OSCAR: Of course it's true. He has a life ahead of him, and my days have suddenly become numbered. Why should he give up what's his for me? What right do I have to ask that of him? Love? Surely, love, too, has its limits before it sours into impassivity, apathy, and hate.

MING: Listen, I want to take care of you.

OSCAR: You can't even take care of yourself.

MING: I love you.

OSCAR: Please don't.

MING: But I do.

OSCAR: I—know. Just don't. Okay?

MING: Why are you doing this then?

OSCAR: It's for the best.

MING: There's nothing I can say to—

OSCAR: Nothing at all. Please don't—

MING: What will I do?

OSCAR: I don't know.

MING: I'll move out.

OSCAR: You don't have to.

MING: It'll be easier.

OSCAR: You can wait until—

MING: Tomorrow.

OSCAR: You can stay until you find—

MING: I'll stay with a friend.

OSCAR: You really don't have to rush—

MING: I want to.

OSCAR: Then the silence.

MING: There's really nothing left to say. Even between friends.

OSCAR: He's angry. I'm upset. Maybe I was wrong to break it off. Some people like to rehearse their speeches, say the right things, use the right words, wear the right color-coordinated clothes, put on the right music—put on a Broadway production just to ease the pain. Maybe I should have rehearsed. Soft lighting might have helped. But what good will it do? I'm lousy at beating around the bush. Just say it. Straight to the point. The facts. Over and done. There's no easy way to end a relationship.

MING: Maybe this is what I really need. A fresh start. A fresh break.

OSCAR: He's probably depressed. I know, deep inside, this is for the best. It is. It is. I know it is.

MING: A thousand thoughts exploding in my mind. Moving. Packing. A new apartment. Maybe roommates. New phone number. Explaining to everyone why I'm moving out. Dating again. Loneliness.

OSCAR: I just want to say that you mean a lot—

MING: Don't.

OSCAR: The last four years were—

MING: Can you be an asshole and make this easier for me?

OSCAR: Do you want some tea? I—I'm having a cup.

MING: Yeah. The usual.

OSCAR: Cookie?

MING: Uh-huh.

OSCAR: It won't be a moment.

MING: We were polite even when we broke up. We've always been so fucking polite to each other. Please. Thank you. You're welcome. After you. I guess we were both afraid to offend each other, to see each other in the real light, to lose one another. Now we have nothing to lose.

OSCAR: I see no reason to start a fight.

MING: We never fought. Maybe that's why. We should have fought regularly. About small things. About big things. Lay things out on the table. Express ourselves. Release the anger instead of bottling everything inside. Like every couple.

OSCAR: Like every American couple.

MING: Like every normal couple.

OSCAR: My father used to beat me with his fists, when I didn't get the perfect grade in school. Once I failed English. I was ten. I didn't understand my tenses—couldn't get them right—got them all mixed up—past, present, perfect, continuous. That night, with a whip in his hand and the test paper in another, my father caned me. And in a consuming rage, he struck me in the left eye. The next day, I went to school half blind. My left eye was covered with a patchy white cream. The pain didn't bother me. The embarrassed, silent looks from my friends did. Fighting and violence didn't solve a thing even if I got an A in my next English test. Now, I correct my father's English. Most of the time—deliberately.

MING: I want to fight.

OSCAR: I don't.

MING: Scream. Shout. Throw things.

OSCAR: Then we'll have to replace them.

MING: Talk. We should at least talk.

OSCAR: You know I'm no good at talking.

MING: You're not good at expressing your feelings.

OSCAR: Let's not bring this up again. You know that—

MING: Why not?

OSCAR: Because—

MING: Why the fuck not?

OSCAR: I don't like it when you are—

MING: Let's talk about this—

OSCAR: No.

MING: I want to.

OSCAR: You're getting ridiculous—

MING: I want to. I want to. I want to.

OSCAR: We were in the kitchen. Cooking dinner.

MING: Come on. Let's hear your stupid fucking reason again.

OSCAR: I was dicing tomatoes. I pretended I didn't hear a word.

MING: You're always like this. Always. When you don't want to talk, you just clam up. Keep quiet. I hate it. Hate it.

OSCAR: All I could think of was the image of a little boy with a patchy white cream on his left eye and his angry father. I kept dicing the tomatoes. Into smaller pieces.

MING: Did you hear me? I hate it when you do this.

OSCAR: He got carried away. He started talking. Loudly.

MING: I was yelling.

OSCAR: Screaming.

MING: I got frustrated. Angry. Trapped.

OSCAR: He threw things around when his words finally failed him. Pots. Pans. Dishes. Glasses. Tomatoes. From the kitchen counter. Into the air. Onto the kitchen floor. A mess. A loud mess.

MING: He kept silent. Not looking at me. Looking at the floor.

OSCAR: Dented pots. Pieces of glass shattered into a thousand pieces. Tomato slices all over the floor.

MING: Then he methodically cleaned the floor. Without a sound. Later, we never mentioned the incident again. Acted as if nothing happened.

OSCAR: It happened once. And never again. Fighting solves nothing.

MING: He's not good at expressing his feelings.

OSCAR: You know the reason.

MING: You're Chinese. You're supposed to be lousy at expressing yourself.

OSCAR: Words don't come easily.

MING: I'm a Chink, too.

OSCAR: I wish you'd stop that.

MING: Stop what?

OSCAR: You know.

MING: Chink?

OSCAR: I hate it when you use that. It's—

MING: Offensive.

OSCAR: Self-debasing.

MING: Ooh. Big word.

OSCAR: Racist. Please don't use that word in front of me.

MING: Chink?

OSCAR: You're not really Chinese, anyway, so what would you know about—

MING: What do you mean by that?

OSCAR: Nothing.

MING: Tell me.

OSCAR: Forget it.

MING: Say it.

OSCAR: You're of a different type.

MING: Of Chinese? Meaning?

OSCAR: You're an ABC.

MING: Labels. Boxes. Categories.

OSCAR: American-born Chinese.

MING: So?

OSCAR: You know what I mean.

MING: I'm a banana. Another category.

OSCAR: Yellow on the outside. White on the inside.

MING: I can't order anything in a Chinese restaurant. I know what the food looks like. What it tastes like. But I just don't know what the fuck it is. What it is called. Of course, it doesn't help if I try describing it in English to the waiters. All I get is a dish that is completely different from what I want, and vile looks. It's as if I have committed some kind of cultural rape, a racial sacrilege. And if I try to order with the pathetic string of elementary Cantonese words every Caucasian tourist in Chinatown knows, they mutter and defiantly speak broken English to me. My Chinese is unbearable to them.

OSCAR: I always order for the two of us.

MING: He does that because I embarrass him.

OSCAR: I do that because you always order the same thing. I thought we'd order something different. That's all.

MING: I don't know when I stopped learning how to speak Chinese. Must be in grade school. Everyone at school spoke English beautifully, and my English was always—well, unrefined, pidgin, tainted. The stuff Rex Harrison sang of in *My Fair Lady*. When I saw the movie, I felt I was Audrey Hepburn. More than anything else in the world, I wanted to be like her: delicate, refined, speaking perfectly, and wearing a Cecil Beaton original. Since no one at home spoke English fluently, I would spend countless hours watching TV every day. Repeating the same lines after Connie Chung and Mary Tyler Moore until I got the pronunciation, the rhythms, the expressions all down pat. My mother thought I was insane. But I finally did speak English just like everyone else, if not better. I think *My Fair Lady* was pivotal in my life. It taught me how to speak proper English, appreciate good clothes, and made me realize I was gay.

OSCAR: Let's not talk about this.

MING: About what?

OSCAR: About who's more Chinese and who isn't.

MING: There you go again. Changing the subject. Shying away from confrontation.

OSCAR: I don't know why we stay together sometimes. He infuriates me. He's the complete antithesis of who and what I am. Yet I need him. Without him, I'm incomplete. Empty.

MING: I feel the same way. We're opposite poles.

OSCAR: The only thing that truly binds us together is being Chinese.

MING: The only thing that truly pits us against each other is being Chinese.

OSCAR: And he's always contradicting me.

MING: You never hold me.

OSCAR: In public, I don't.

MING: Kiss me.

OSCAR: Not here.

MING: Why not?

OSCAR: What I feel for you is private. Between us. Not some crude display for the rest of the world to see.

MING: I've often felt the urge to put my tongue into his mouth in public. To shock? For effect? I don't know.

OSCAR: For effect.

MING: You never said you loved me.

OSCAR: I have.

MING: When?

OSCAR: In my own little way.

MING: It's not enough.

OSCAR: I'm not the type who has to remind you of my feelings constantly.

MING: I need to hear it. Constantly. It makes me feel—wanted. Needed.

OSCAR: My father and mother have never said they loved me. My friends are the same. It's our way.

MING: Another excuse.

OSCAR: We show our affections through deeds. Through actions. When I got a Lego set for my seventh birthday, I knew I was very loved. All thirty-five dollars and seventy-six cents of love. That's why some people see the Chinese as materialistic. You know someone is well loved when they're driving a Mercedes-Benz.

MING: I think I can live on that kind of love.

OSCAR: Sometimes I wish I could hug him freely. Touch him, hold him whenever I want to. Instinctively. And I need that touch, too. The funny thing is that it's the same physical touch that repels me. Makes me uncomfortable. Awkward. Vulnerable.

MING: You're not demonstrative.

OSCAR: Being physically demonstrative is very difficult for me.

MING: How difficult can it be? You haven't tried. Come.

(MING *opens his arms to* OSCAR.)

OSCAR: What?

MING: Come here.

OSCAR: This is stupid.

MING: Hold me.

OSCAR: I can't.

MING: Come on.

OSCAR: Stop it.

MING: Forget it. You are right as usual. It was stupid.

OSCAR: I don't know when was the last time I held my father, kissed my mother. It just isn't done. Sometimes I want to, especially when I see how my American friends behave toward their loved ones. Hugging and kissing. When I was young, I often wished that I was born into the Partridge Family or the Brady Bunch. They were always smiling, laughing, doing all those tactile kinds of things—

MING: Tactile—

OSCAR: As in touching—

MING: Why can't you use simple words? You always complicate—

OSCAR: As I was saying, when I see my parents, I automatically keep a respectful distance. Because it's a part of our upbringing and because it's expected. Are you physical with your parents?

MING: No.

OSCAR: So why are you singling me out?

MING: My parents, in case you forgot, are not speaking to me.

OSCAR: That's not the point.

MING: That's precisely the point. I came out to them.

OSCAR: That was a very intelligent thing to do.

MING: I didn't want to lie to them. They are my parents, for Christ's sake.

OSCAR: Not anymore.

MING: At least I don't have to lie to my folks about having no time to date because I'm busy at work.

OSCAR: You should have understood where your parents were coming from. They may live here in the U.S., but their ways are still of China.

MING: Mine aren't.

OSCAR: This is one of the reasons I'm so madly attracted to him. His questioning. His challenges. It's also one of the reasons I feel compelled to swing an axe into his forehead every now and then.

MING: I hated his line of reasoning. It's so logical. So rational. No other way, except the right way. His way. Sometimes I think I'm fucking Mr. Spock.

OSCAR: We've known each other for some time now.

MING: We've been seeing each other for four years.

OSCAR: Four years, two months, three weeks, and four days, to be exact. We were lovers.

MING: I always hated that word. Lovers. It's so—

OSCAR: Committed.

MING: No.

OSCAR: Ambiguous.

MING: Yes.

OSCAR: What about companion?

MING: Roommate.

OSCAR: Boyfriend.

MING: Sex toy?

OSCAR: Husband and wife?

MING: Friends.

OSCAR: We lived together.

MING: Slept together.

OSCAR: Ate together.

MING: Watched TV together.

OSCAR: Spent countless weekends at Ikea. Rummaging through bins of turquoise plastic utensils we bought but never used.

MING: Spent countless hours at Tower Records. Buying CDs we never played.

OSCAR: Years of dancing in the living room on quiet afternoons.

MING: Years of wearing each other's underwear.

OSCAR: Years of tolerating each other's friends.

MING: Borrowing and stealing each other's vocabulary.

OSCAR: "Way cool."

MING: "Tactile."

OSCAR: Observing each other's idiosyncrasies change from cute little gestures to annoying habits.

MING: Years of loving each other.

OSCAR: And hating each other.

MING: Years of quietly sitting beside each other without having to exchange a word.

OSCAR: Him reading. And I watching him.

MING: We were the perfect couple.

OSCAR: We never quarreled. Never fought.

MING: Sometimes we should have. But we never did.

OSCAR: I was very happy.

MING: I was—happy.

OSCAR: Then things change. Like they always do.

MING: He got sick.

OSCAR: AIDS.

MING: Sick.

OSCAR: I had the flu that wouldn't go away.

MING: The warning bells were ringing. Loudly. But I said, Hey, you're just paranoid. Nothing a couple of aspirins can't fix.

OSCAR: I felt tired.

MING: No night sweats. No lesions. No nothing. It's only a cold. Keep calm.

OSCAR: So I went to the doctor.

MING: Why? It's only a cold. Everyone gets a cold.

OSCAR: He gave me a whole slew of tests.

MING: It's a cold.

OSCAR: I tested positive.

MING: He was sick. Sick.

OSCAR: I tried to persuade him to take the test.

MING: I don't have a cold.

OSCAR: That's not the issue here.

MING: I'm not tired.

OSCAR: You have to find out—

MING: Do I look sick?

OSCAR: Go.

MING: I couldn't.

OSCAR: You must.

MING: Later.

OSCAR: Why are you so hesitant?

MING: Why don't you leave me alone?

OSCAR: Are you afraid that you might be—

MING: Sick.

OSCAR: HIV positive.

MING: Sick.

OSCAR: Positive.

MING: Sick is a better word.

OSCAR: But it has the same meaning.

MING: I don't know why you keep volleying, ramming the words AIDS and HIV positive down my throat. It's like you're almost fucking proud to wear the label around your neck. I hate it. I hate it.

OSCAR: But it's the truth.

MING: He likes categorizing people. Boxing things into their rightful places. This is white. This is Asian. This is gay. This is straight. And this is what you're fucking supposed to do when you're in this category. He organizes people like he organizes his office.

OSCAR: It's just easier for me to deal with life this way. Okay?

MING: What if I'm positive?

OSCAR: We were always safe, weren't we?

MING: What if the condom tore?

OSCAR: Was the lubricant water-based?

MING: Were we ever irresponsible? Forgot about safe sex in the heat of passion or when we had too much to drink?

OSCAR: After persuading him.

MING: Nagging.

OSCAR: He finally went.

MING: Waiting for the results almost crippled me for a week. Kept me wondering—What if? What if? I started to write a will. Who'd get the CDs? Who'd get my books? It's so morbid. I'm not even fucking thirty!

OSCAR: I did the same. What should I give him? What do you give someone you love after you die? Perhaps memories, photographs, strange obscure objects that have significant meaning—even those things get lost eventually. He tested negative.

MING: Thank God.

OSCAR: He only believed in God when it was convenient. Only when he wanted things. Like a car phone or a leather jacket.

MING: I suddenly felt free. Like I've been given wings. To fly.

OSCAR: I am happy for him. I am. Yet I felt a little left behind. A little betrayed.

MING: Then it got uncomfortable.

OSCAR: We got uncomfortable.

MING: We had nothing to say to each other.

OSCAR: If we did, the word that lingered at the tip of our tongues was AIDS.

MING: If we didn't, we thought it. Loudly.

OSCAR: We stopped having sex. With each other.

MING: All of a sudden, I couldn't bear his touch.

OSCAR: We began spending strenuous hours in the apartment in our own different worlds.

MING: Sat beside each other without exchanging a word.

OSCAR: Me wanting to be closer.

MING: Me wanting to be as far away as possible.

OSCAR: And I knew.

MING: We avoided each other like the plague.

OSCAR: That was a poor choice of words.

MING: I didn't mean it.

OSCAR: Right.

MING: Really.

OSCAR: Thoughts swirl in my mind: Maybe his results were botched. Maybe the test didn't detect the virus. Did he infect me? Did he fuck around? I didn't.

MING: I thought the same thing.

OSCAR: Maybe it was someone else. Years ago. Before I met him.

MING: A quick moment.

OSCAR: A brief encounter with a hastily scribbled telephone number on a piece of paper as a souvenir.

MING: Or a harmless fling in Montreal with a Jean-Pierre, Jean-Luc, Jean-Claude, or Jean-something.

OSCAR: The summer vacation you took without me.

MING: You said it was healthy we took separate vacations. Expand our horizons, you said.

OSCAR: But I didn't say you could—

MING: Exactly.

OSCAR: I have been faithful since we started seeing each other.

MING: I slipped. Every now and then. So I'm human. Sometimes I wondered if I should have been the one who was sick.

OSCAR: We got further away from each other.

MING: Deliberately.

OSCAR: Naturally.

MING: It was then I realized that I wasn't strong. The sickness tested our relationship, and I wasn't passing with flying colors like I ought to.

OSCAR: I became his obstacle, his wet blanket.

MING: I slept around more. A little more. Discreetly, of course.

OSCAR: He came back from work later than usual.

MING: Meetings.

OSCAR: I see. Do you want dinner?

MING: I had something to eat. Before I came home.

OSCAR: I see.

MING: I'm tired.

OSCAR: Long day?

MING: Yeah.

OSCAR: I see.

MING: I'm going to bed.

OSCAR: Good night.

MING: Yeah.

OSCAR: I can usually tolerate harmless indiscretions. I turn a blind eye. Pretend it doesn't happen. So why is it worrying me now?

MING: Jealousy?

OSCAR: Were his casual relationships more than physical? Was he getting emotionally involved with someone else?

MING: During this time, I slept around with many different men. But every time I was having sex, I saw only his face. Heard his urgent moans. Felt his smooth, hot body against mine. Then I'd stop. Get up and leave.

OSCAR: I—masturbated—thinking of him when we were both still—happy.

MING: You just don't turn me on anymore.

OSCAR: I gathered.

MING: I keep thinking of death when—

OSCAR: Please.

MING: I wanted to—

OSCAR: I know.

MING: I wanted to leave.

OSCAR: Then leave.

MING: But I can't.

OSCAR: Why not?

MING: Because I want to look after you.

OSCAR: You feel responsible.

MING: Perhaps.

OSCAR: Guilty.

MING: Maybe.

OSCAR: Afraid of what our friends are going to say if you leave?

MING: That, too. Yes.

OSCAR: Then I'll make it easier for the both of us.

MING: How?

OSCAR: I don't think we should see each other anymore.

MING: We'll be friends.

OSCAR: Good friends.

MING: It seems so long ago.

OSCAR: What seems so long ago?

MING: When we first met.

OSCAR: Yes. Doesn't it?

MING: Do you remember how it happened?

OSCAR: Some dinner party on Charles Street.

MING: I thought it was in the South End.

OSCAR: Some gay Asian party with lots of French hors d'oeuvres.

MING: Yellow creamy seafood droppings on water crackers that look like they should hang on an earlobe with a skimpy black dress, instead of dripping on the side of your mouth.

OSCAR: A typical Asian-wanna-be-Caucasian-and-Caucasian-wanna-be-in-Asian kind of party.

MING: Everyone at the party was frantically speaking in tongues.

OSCAR: Thai, Cantonese, Vietnamese, Tagalog, pig Latin. And believe it or not, French.

MING: The Americans were looking rather bewildered. Sat there politely complimenting the host and deciphering what the hell they were eating. Nodding too frequently and sometimes a little too enthusiastically at anyone who wasn't white. Arching their eyebrows at everyone white as if to say, "Where am I?"

OSCAR: While all this was going on, I stood by the kitchen looking at him across the room.

MING: Staring.

OSCAR: I wondered at that moment what it was like to kiss you.

MING: To see you naked.

OSCAR: To run my fingers down your chest.

MING: I wondered if you had a big cock.

OSCAR: But we never spoke to each other.

MING: Instead, we talked to the people around us halfheartedly. Pretending to smile. Pretending to be engaged in conversation while we stole glances at each other every opportunity we got.

OSCAR: We couldn't get away.

MING: I was with friends.

OSCAR: I was with a date.

MING: And I desperately wanted to lose them.

OSCAR: I wanted to shoot my date fatally. I thought that would constitute a logical reason to excuse myself to walk toward him.

MING: It must be an ancient Chinese mating ritual. Never speaking to people you desire to have wild sex and a meaningful relationship with. That's why it was easier to prearrange marriages in the old days. You know, the ritual of binding feet was not an indication of the breeding of fine Chinese women. No, parents bound their daughters' feet so they couldn't run away from their pre-chosen spouses. They'd have to fucking hop like mad to run away. Right now, I'd love to bind his feet. Chinese S&M.

OSCAR: The Chinese can be shy.

MING: You should make the first move. Come over, accidentally spill a drink on me. Apologize profusely but never for once take your glance off me. Compliment me. Write your phone number on a paper napkin and slip it in my pocket.

OSCAR: You should have. After all, you were the whiter one. The more physically demonstrative one.

MING: Anyway, I got a call from him the next day.

OSCAR: I got his number from the host.

MING: We arranged to meet for dinner the following evening.

OSCAR: How about Ciao Bella on Newberry Street?

MING: Sure.

OSCAR: Dinner in a small Italian restaurant.

MING: At first, it was rather awkward.

OSCAR: So—did you enjoy the party?

MING: Yeah.

OSCAR: Trying to make polite conversation.

MING: We talked.

OSCAR: In circles.

MING: About the unpredictable New England weather.

OSCAR: About politics.

MING: About people whom we have in common. People we know. People we didn't want to know.

OSCAR: About Madonna's latest CD and its political significance on Asians in America.

MING: About his name. Oscar. Asians always pick out the most curious and most discarded English names from books and TV. Like Cornelius. Elmo. Wellington. They do it to assimilate into the American culture.

OSCAR: Oscar is easier to pronounce. I've had my Chinese name massacred all too frequently by strangers and friends. And his name? Ming. It's not even his real name. He picked up a Chinese name because he wanted to be in touch with his cultural roots. Picking up a name is not like picking up a culture.

MING: All the while, I was mentally undressing him.

OSCAR: All the while, I was wondering what it was like to stroke your cheek.

MING: I kept looking at you.

OSCAR: You were beautiful.

MING: Mature.

OSCAR: Intelligent.

MING: Polite.

OSCAR: Talkative.

MING: We ate.

OSCAR: And talked again.

MING: After dinner, we walked around for a while.

OSCAR: Peered into brightly lit shop windows.

MING: Sat on the steps of an old church in Copley Square.

OSCAR: Looking at young couples walking by.

MING: Looking at old couples on park benches.

OSCAR: Looking at each other.

MING: Then you asked me back. To your place.

OSCAR: Hope—I'm not—being too—

MING: No—

OSCAR: I'm not usually—

MING: I know—

OSCAR: I really—like you.

MING: I kept thinking: Will he respect me in the morning? Should I care whether he respects me?

OSCAR: My apartment is a mess. I should have vacuumed. Lemon Pledged. Something.

MING: Fuck, I'm wearing contact lenses. Maybe he's got some saline. What if he doesn't? Then I'm fucked.

OSCAR: I've got to get up early tomorrow. Work. What am I doing?

MING: If I go back to his apartment, he might think I'm a slut.

OSCAR: Is he a slut?

MING: It's not like this crosses my mind every time I go back with someone. But I kinda like him, and I really don't want to fuck this up because I want to—I want this to be right.

OSCAR: So we took a cab.

MING: Back to his apartment in Brookline.

OSCAR: And made love.

MING: On the staircase.

OSCAR: In the cold bedroom above.

MING: Yes.

OSCAR: Again and again.

MING: Yes.

OSCAR: Then you moved in.

MING: For four years.

OSCAR: We discovered new uses for the kitchen and the living room.

MING: Acted like children in museums on Sundays.

OSCAR: Read poetry in my large wooden bed by candlelight.

MING: Had breakfast in Union Park.

OSCAR: Secretly held hands on crowded Boston streets.

MING: You were always embarrassed to hold hands in public.

OSCAR: I wasn't.

MING: Instead, you let me hold your finger.

OSCAR: Yes. Sometimes.

MING: Not your hand.

OSCAR: Sometimes my hand.

MING: Sometimes.

OSCAR: Holding hands on subway trains to Brookline after work.

MING: Chasing after trains that are never on time.

OSCAR: Do you know how many trains we sat on together?

OSCAR: Seemed like thousands.

OSCAR: And I thought—in thousands more.

MING: Four years.

OSCAR: Four years.

(MING *goes over to* OSCAR *and they kiss passionately.*)

OSCAR: Yes. (*Pause.*) Ming?

MING: Yes?

OSCAR: I—want to say—I—

MING: Yes.

OSCAR: I—I—uh—nothing. It's nothing.

(*A beat.*)

MING (*disappointed*): I see. (*Pause.*) Then one night when I came home, you said—

OSCAR: I don't think we should see each other anymore.

MING: I didn't know what to say. I stood there as if someone had slapped me in the face.

OSCAR: I had to say it.

MING: I was hurt. Bruised. Stunned. I knew this was going to happen, and I even thought about it. But when it really happens, it just takes your breath away. All the time, rehearsing, thinking, plotting, doesn't matter. It's the moment, that moment, that does.

OSCAR: Maybe I just wanted to say it before he did.

MING: I laid my brown coat and leather briefcase down on the wood floor.

OSCAR: It was very difficult for me as well. You know that, don't you?

MING: Let's not talk. Okay?

OSCAR: I want you to know—

MING: Shh—shh—

OSCAR: Okay.

MING: So I moved out.

OSCAR: Is this Donna Summer CD yours or mine?

MING: Yours. *La Traviata, Turandot, Carmen.* All the classical stuff—yours.

OSCAR: Pet Shop Boys—

MING: Mine—

OSCAR: Pet Shop Boys—

MING: Mine—

OSCAR: Pet Shop Boys—

MING: Mine. All mine.

OSCAR: And this?

MING: Yours.

OSCAR: Mine.

MING: Uh-huh.

OSCAR: I don't know what I was feeling as I saw him pack his things away. Quietly and methodically. Breakables in one. Books in another. Perhaps he's right. I should express what I feel. Say what I think. But how can I express something when I don't know what I feel? I want to say don't go, but I know I'm doing the right thing.

MING: The usual anger.

OSCAR: Silence.

MING: Sadness.

OSCAR: The process of lovers becoming friends.

MING: The process all civilized ex-lovers go through.

OSCAR: Here.

MING: What is it?

OSCAR: Satie.

MING: Keep it.

OSCAR: It's yours.

MING: You've always liked it.

OSCAR: I couldn't.

MING: I want you to have it. You like it more than I ever did.

OSCAR: Thanks.

MING: Books.

OSCAR: Underwear.

MING: Kitchen utensils.

OSCAR: Bed sheets.

MING: Toiletries.

OSCAR: All divided.

MING: All sorted into nice, little, brown boxes.

OSCAR: Our lives in the past four years packed neatly in boxes.

MING: The room was empty.

OSCAR: Listen, I want us to be friends.

MING: Sure.

OSCAR: And if you need anything, please call.

MING: I know.

OSCAR: Anything at all. I insist.

MING: So fucking amiable.

OSCAR: He won't call.

MING: I won't call.

OSCAR: Call me when you're settled in.

MING: The first night after I moved out, I got myself drunk with warm beer and quickly fell into the warm, sturdy arms of a handsome waiter.

OSCAR: I sat home and watched *Seinfeld*. Wondering if I had done the right thing. Wondering if he was all right. Wondering if I had made a very bad mistake. Wondering why everyone thought *Seinfeld* was funny. Wondering.

MING: I was thinking about you while making love to the waiter.

OSCAR: I watched TV until one. I didn't know what I was watching.

MING: I made love to this stranger who smelled of coffee and roast chicken the same way I made love to you. The exact order. The exact style. But the stranger's moans and whispers weren't yours.

OSCAR: How was he? Where was he? What was he doing?

MING: Three weeks later, I moved in with the waiter. His name is Robert.

OSCAR: Will he call? Shall I call? Call me.

MING: Robert's a head waiter in some fancy restaurant downtown.

OSCAR: After moping around for a month, I started dating again. At first I got in touch with a group of people who were HIV positive. In that group there was a whole different world of gay men, people who had different priorities than going to clubs or the gym. We met twice a week and talked about what things are like now that we're HIV positive. Personally, I don't see any difference. My pay is still the same. My lover is still gone. I don't club much anyway. The best analogy for being positive is losing your boyfriend. Losing a part of you you took for granted. You're still the same, but never whole, not completely. In the group, there was a new vocabulary, a new language, discussions on T-cells, AZT and PCP, vegetarian picnics on Sundays, jazz bowling on Tuesdays, and advanced macramé classes on Thursdays—but I soon tired of it. I just wondered what he was doing. How he was getting along.

MING: I fell in love with Robert. Sometimes I wondered if I was on the rebound. Or just emotionally needy.

OSCAR: Then I heard from some of my friends that he had been seen with a white guy in a bar. All over each other. Kissing, holding hands in public. Said he looked happy. Not happier, just happy.

MING: I heard he spends most of his time alone. It would be nice to hear he'd gotten out and started dating. Seeing other people. Or something. On the other hand, I think it would make me upset to know that he was dating someone else. I don't know what I think or feel anymore. I don't want to think or feel. Just be. Be myself. I don't know who or what I am. Without him.

OSCAR: I started meeting people again. Being positive is one thing. Knowing that he's dating again and being happy is another.

MING: Six months flew by. And not a word.

OSCAR: Then one day when I got home from work, I saw a letter in his handwriting. He sent me a birthday card. But no present.

MING: He sent me a Christmas card. Typed. Very cordial. Detached. Like it was sent by a bank or an insurance company.

OSCAR: Then silence.

MING: Just the other day, I got a message on my phone machine.

OSCAR: Hi. It's—uh—me. Listen, I'm having a little party this Saturday and would like—you to come. Can you? It'd be great to catch up with you again. It's nothing fancy. Some of the old gang will be there. They'd love to see you. Really. I hope you can come. Bring your—friend—or any friend along. (*Pause.*) Bye.

MING: My heart started beating wildly.

OSCAR: Maybe I'm curious to see who replaced me.

MING: I started playing his message over and over again. Hearing his voice. Trying to read between the lines. I was already coordinating my clothes for the party in my head.

OSCAR: I wondered if we'd be friendly and civil to each other. I wondered if he'd show up at all.

MING: I thought it'd be nice to see him again.

OSCAR: After all these months.

MING: I wanted to see his boyfriend.

OSCAR: And I, his.

MING: I wanted to see him.

OSCAR: Yes.

MING: The party was just that—a party. About forty people once again crammed into a Boston apartment speaking wildly in tongues. Like an evangelical convention.

OSCAR: I saw him come into the apartment with his friend and I immediately ran into the kitchen. I don't know why. But I did. My cheeks were flushed red. I stood there, pretending to arrange food by color hues—orange with reds, blues with purples, on and on.

MING: Where could he be?

OSCAR: I came out. Finally. Excited and nervous. Carrying a fruit tray.

MING: Hi.

OSCAR: Hi.

MING: You look great.

OSCAR: You do, too.

MING: Like your new hairstyle.

OSCAR: Silence.

MING: This is Robert.

OSCAR: Hi.

MING: He's wearing that shirt I got him when we were on the Cape last year. I wonder if it's deliberate. Trying to guilt me or something.

OSCAR: Robert is very good looking. I can see them both naked, making love on the kitchen floor. Our kitchen floor.

MING: Nice party.

OSCAR: What?

MING: Nice party.

OSCAR: Oh, thanks.

MING: I shouldn't look at him too much; otherwise, Robert will get funny ideas, and then we'll have another drama at home.

OSCAR: Let me get both of you a drink.

MING: Bet he knows what drink to get me without asking. Habits die hard.

OSCAR: I have this sudden urge to kiss him.

MING: He has no visible signs of being HIV positive.

OSCAR: Why is he looking at me that way?

MING: He is a little thinner. But still as handsome.

OSCAR: I wish Robert wasn't that good looking. It would be easier for me to know that he's been sleeping with a troll.

MING: There were people I hadn't seen in ages.

OSCAR: The party was large enough to get lost in but small enough to know he was around somewhere.

MING: We were looking at each other again.

OSCAR: Across the room.

MING: But not directly. Fleeting glances.

OSCAR: Like the first time we met.

MING: I finally met his Asian friend through some old friends of mine. Quite a nice guy. Amusing in his own little way. I'm glad for the both of them. Or aren't I?

OSCAR: Robert is a nice man. Charming, personable, smart, good looking. He must have some flaw. Maybe he has a small dick. He must have.

MING: I saw him slip into the bedroom. I'm sure he looked in my direction.

OSCAR: I don't know if I did it deliberately.

MING: I excused myself.

OSCAR: I hoped he'd seen me walk in here.

MING: There you are.

OSCAR: Here I am.

MING: I was looking for you.

OSCAR: Really?

MING: Yes.

OSCAR: I'm here.

MING: So you are. (*Pause.*) Everything's exactly the way it was.

OSCAR: Uh-huh.

MING: Nothing changed.

OSCAR: Why? Should it?

MING: No.

OSCAR: I don't know why I'm getting defensive.

MING: Maybe I should just hightail it the fuck out of here.

OSCAR: You said you were looking for me?

MING: Yeah. I wanted to talk to you.

OSCAR: About what?

MING: Nothing in particular.

OSCAR: Just the usual pleasantries, then.

MING: What do ex-lovers talk about?

OSCAR: Are you happy with Robert?

MING: Do I want to talk about Robert and me?

OSCAR: Talk about us. How we used to be. How we still can be.

MING: Do I want to talk about his new friend? Do I want to talk about us? Do I want to talk?

OSCAR: I want to pin him down on the bed and rape him like a Sabine woman.

MING: A what woman?

OSCAR: Sabine.

MING: What's that?

OSCAR: It's—forget it.

MING: Tell me.

OSCAR: The moment's lost.

MING: Now what? Do I touch him?

OSCAR: Like the way you used to. Instinctively. Automatically. Without question or hesitation.

MING: Do I hold him? Hug him? Kiss him?

OSCAR: The harmless gestures we once took for granted. The casual and familiar actions that became second nature to us. These old habits now hold different meanings and interpretations. All of a sudden, we've become two awkward strangers in a cold room. Wrestling with a new, unspeakable language that belongs only to old lovers.

MING: So why are you here?

OSCAR: Because I want to be.

MING: Is something wrong?

OSCAR: No.

MING: I know you.

OSCAR: So?

MING: Your health?

OSCAR: It's fine. My T's are up.

MING: Your what?

OSCAR: Nothing.

MING: Boyfriend?

OSCAR: No.

MING: Family? Not your father again?

OSCAR: No.

MING: Someone you want to avoid out there?

OSCAR: Maybe.

MING: I knew it. I shouldn't have come.

OSCAR: Forget it. I shouldn't have said anything.

MING: I knew coming here was a mistake.

OSCAR: I wanted you to come. You and Robert. Both of you.

MING: I know, but it's just too soon.

OSCAR: It's not.

MING: I'll go. I'll get Robert, and we'll both go.

OSCAR: Don't.

MING: I think it's—

OSCAR: Stay. I want you to stay.

MING: Assertion and aggression. Quite a change.

OSCAR: I want to tell him so many things. The things I've been thinking, feeling. But it's difficult.

MING: Seems so long ago.

OSCAR: What seems so long ago?

MING: My being in here.

OSCAR: Yes.

MING: The nights, the afternoons in here.

OSCAR: Making love.

MING: Smoking French cigarettes.

OSCAR: Lying next to each other. Not talking.

MING: Never wanting to leave the room except to take a quick leak.

OSCAR: Listening to Satie. Reading the Sunday papers together.

MING: Telling each other secrets.

OSCAR: Secrets he's now sharing with his new friend.

MING: I've run out of conversation. Out of words.

OSCAR: I want to kiss you. Gently on your soft lips.

MING: You know, there are mornings when I wake up thinking I'm here. The bay windows, wood floors, candles, and the cat purring on top of me.

OSCAR: What does he mean by that?

MING: Why did I say that?

OSCAR: He wants me.

MING: He must think I'm flirting with him.

OSCAR: He's flirting with me.

MING: You should be out there.

OSCAR: Why?

MING: You're the host. You should be mingling, introducing people, asking if they want more food, drink, I don't know. Out there. Not here.

OSCAR: I want to be here. For a while, anyway.

MING: I'm getting aroused.

OSCAR: Come sit on the bed.

MING: Should I sit on the bed?

OSCAR: Sit.

MING: No. It's okay. I'll just stand.

OSCAR: Come on, sit.

MING: It'll be too awkward.

OSCAR: Sit.

MING: I wonder if Robert is looking for me.

OSCAR: Sit.

MING: I'll sit.

OSCAR: Thank you, God.

MING: I haven't seen these people in such a long time.

OSCAR: Sit closer.

MING: So many familiar faces.

OSCAR: Closer.

(MING *sits closer to* OSCAR.)

MING: Am I sitting too close?

OSCAR: You should have called them.

MING: It isn't the same.

OSCAR: What do you mean?

MING: They're your friends.

OSCAR: His knee is touching mine. Oh, Jesus.

MING: I'm being too coy. Think about Robert. Think about what Mother looks like naked. Think about what Jesus looks like naked.

OSCAR: Fuck, he's pulling away.

MING: I'm getting uncomfortable.

OSCAR: They were your friends, too.

MING: Yeah, but you knew them longer.

OSCAR: That's not the point.

MING: After we broke up, it's natural they took your side.

OSCAR: That's ridiculous.

MING: They blame me, don't they?

OSCAR: Blame you for what?

MING: Us.

OSCAR: No.

MING: They blame me. I can see it in their eyes.

OSCAR: They like you.

MING: Sure.

OSCAR: They always ask about you.

MING: Gossips.

OSCAR: After all, I was the one responsible for the breakup, remember?

MING: Yes. You were.

OSCAR: I wish we didn't break up. If I could just make it right again. Wish I never did what I did. Wish it all never happened. And we're here together again.

MING: How's work?

OSCAR: Good. How's your work?

MING: The usual. Busy.

OSCAR: I see.

MING: I'm going to Venice next week. On business.

OSCAR: We always wanted to go to Venice together. Gondolas in sleepy canals.

MING: He said he wanted to retire there.

OSCAR: We never did it, did we? Venice. Another regret. Now, he's probably going to Venice with Robert. Doing things we always wanted to do there.

MING: I'll be there for four days.

OSCAR: Venice should be very nice this time of the year.

MING: Wish you could come with me. Ask me.

OSCAR: We could walk across old bridges and make love in a small pensione in hot afternoons. Take me to Venice with you.

MING: I'm taking Robert with me.

OSCAR: I see. Good.

MING: Are you dating?

OSCAR: Yes and no.

MING: Which?

OSCAR: Yes, I'm dating. No, it's nothing serious.

MING: Anyone in particular?

OSCAR: Yes.

MING: Who?

OSCAR: A Filipino guy.

MING: He's here.

OSCAR: Yeah.

MING: What's his name?

OSCAR: His name is— Why do you want to know?

MING: Just want to know.

OSCAR: His name is Daniel.

MING: I see.

OSCAR: He's young.

MING: I've been replaced by someone younger.

OSCAR: He's nice.

MING: Good. I'm happy for you.

OSCAR: He's not you.

MING: Does he know?

OSCAR: About?

MING: You.

OSCAR: Yes.

MING: Quite a responsibility for someone so young.

OSCAR: We're only dating. Anyway, he manages.

MING: I see. How long have you been—

OSCAR: Dating? Oh, about three weeks. Your friend—

MING: Robert.

OSCAR: Yes. He's—very cute.

MING: He's nice.

OSCAR: He's white.

MING: So?

OSCAR: I thought you never dated white guys.

MING: Well, I am.

OSCAR: I see.

MING: A lot of Asian guys date white guys.

OSCAR: I know all too many.

MING: Is that a problem?

OSCAR: Asians only date white guys—

MING: Please don't—

OSCAR: To assimilate—

MING: That is not fair—

OSCAR: To emulate—

MING: I'm with Robert because I love—

OSCAR: Anyway, I always thought you only dated Asian guys.

MING: It was a phase.

OSCAR: Like homosexuality.

MING: No. Like it was the politically correct thing to do.

OSCAR: I see.

MING: Some Asians only date Asians because—

OSCAR: They find Asians attractive—

MING: And some—

OSCAR: A politically correct thing to do.

MING: You know what I mean—

OSCAR: Like us.

MING: No. Not like us. Can we not do this?

OSCAR: I've been rude. I shouldn't pry.

MING: I hope I'm making him jealous. He must still care if he's jealous.

OSCAR: He's—young.

MING: He's a year older than me.

OSCAR: A waiter?

MING: Head waiter.

OSCAR: Same thing.

MING: Once I wanted him to be aggressive, but that was then.

OSCAR: Which restaurant?

MING: Cafe Orpheus downtown. What does Daniel do?

OSCAR: A student. Majors in—

MING: Business.

OSCAR: Yes. Harvard.

MING: Like every foreign student from Asia.

OSCAR: Who's putting people into boxes now?

MING: Rich parents?

OSCAR: Yes. He's also a committee member of Act-Up.

MING: Really.

OSCAR: He's a radical queer Asian who lives and breathes Sondheim.

MING: He loves me, you know.

OSCAR: Who?

MING: Robert.

OSCAR: Why is he telling me this?

MING: Why am I telling him this?

OSCAR: I'm—happy for you. Really.

MING: Does—Daniel love you?

OSCAR: I think this is a little premature. I mean, we've only gone out a few times.

MING: Oh.

OSCAR: And we haven't had sex or anything.

MING: You kissed.

OSCAR: No.

MING: Am I prying?

OSCAR: I'm not in love with him.

MING: He's in love with him. God, I don't want to hear this.

OSCAR: I'm still in love with you. Tell him.

MING: Well, that put an end to my childish fantasies.

OSCAR: Tell him or he'll go away. Again.

MING: He's being silent again. It's so annoying.

OSCAR: For once, express yourself. Tell him about your feelings.

MING: He's probably thinking about his friend.

OSCAR: I'm not in love with him.

MING: Why not?

OSCAR: Must you ask?

MING: No.

OSCAR: Because—I still—

MING: What?

(*Pause.*)

OSCAR (*muttering*): I still—(*Pause.*)—love you.

MING: I have to get back to the party.

OSCAR: I thought you always liked confrontations. Wanted me to express what I was feeling.

MING: I—have changed.

OSCAR: Become more Chinese?

MING: Maybe.

OSCAR: I should have said it earlier, I know.

MING: It's different now.

OSCAR: Yes, but—

MING: Why did you end our relationship then?

OSCAR: I thought it was for the best.

MING: Best for you?

OSCAR: Best for you.

MING: How do you know what's best for me?

OSCAR: It wouldn't be fair to you. Looking after me when I got sicker. I couldn't bear to see you hating me.

MING: I wouldn't.

OSCAR: You would. Because I would hate myself if I were in your place.

MING: Then you don't know me.

OSCAR: We lived together for four years. I know you all too well.

MING: How dare you make a selfish decision for the both of us without telling me?

OSCAR: It was for the best.

MING: Fuck you. What right do you—

OSCAR: It's past.

MING: Your decision hurt me.

OSCAR: I'm sorry.

MING: I was lost for weeks.

OSCAR: So was I.

MING: And that was supposed to make me feel better?

OSCAR: You could have asked me to stay.

MING: Asked you to stay?

OSCAR: But you didn't.

MING: I don't believe I'm having this conversation.

OSCAR: You don't remember what happened?

MING: I remember every single word.

OSCAR: I don't think we should see each other anymore.

MING: Every single word! I hear it in my head, at the back of my mind, every single day! Like a scratched record playing on the same groove, over and over again! And it hurts every time I hear it!

OSCAR: And you said nothing! (*Softly.*) You just stood there and listened to me. Smiled and walked out of the room.

MING: And what should I have said?

OSCAR: You're the expressive one. You could have asked to stay.

MING: Begged to stay.

OSCAR: No. Just ask. (*Pause.*) This isn't easy for me to say—but I want you back in my life.

MING: As a friend.

OSCAR: More than a friend.

MING: Meaning?

OSCAR: We could start again. From the beginning.

MING: We can't.

OSCAR: Why not?

MING: You know why.

OSCAR: No.

MING: Because it's not the same anymore.

OSCAR: It can be.

MING: What makes you so sure I want to?

OSCAR: I don't know.

MING: We can't go back to the way things were and make everything all right. It's like learning Chinese. Once I started speaking English, I stopped learning how to speak and write Chinese. I dropped my culture for another. And you can't go back. Only forward. And every now and then, you'll remember a few phrases, a few words, the names of a few Chinese dishes. It sounds a little vague, a little romantic. But the language escapes you because you let it go. It's like learning Chinese. Learning to be Chinese.

OSCAR: We can try and make it work this time.

MING: What if I'm not strong enough to be there for you when you're really sick?

OSCAR: I'll take that risk.

MING: It isn't fair to you.

OSCAR: I'll chance it.

MING: No!

OSCAR: Then we're just going to be friends.

MING: Yes.

OSCAR: Just friends.

MING: Yes.

OSCAR: It's not going to be easy.

MING: I know.

OSCAR: Watching you hold someone else the same way you held me.

MING: Yes.

OSCAR: Watching you hold his hand. His finger.

MING: Let me hold your finger.

(MING *holds* OSCAR's *index finger.*)

OSCAR: It hurts me deeply. To see you happy. To see you in love with someone else. I know it's wrong, but I can't help it. I wish it could have been me.

MING: But I love Robert differently.

OSCAR: More. More than me?

MING: No. Differently.

OSCAR: I do want you to be happy. You know that, don't you?

MING: Yes.

OSCAR: It's just—

MING: Difficult.

OSCAR: You're very handsome.

MING: Thanks.

OSCAR: You are.

(OSCAR *suddenly lurches toward* MING *in an attempt to kiss him.*)

MING: Don't.

OSCAR: They won't know.

MING: I don't want to.

OSCAR: I'm asking you now. Stay. Please stay.

MING: There are others involved now. (*Pause.*) No matter what happens, I'm always there for you.

OSCAR: We'll become friends then.

MING: Best friends.

OSCAR: Best friends.

MING: I wish it would have been different.

OSCAR: So do I.

MING: But it can't.

(MING *walks away.*)

OSCAR: I love you.

(MING *stops with his back to* OSCAR.)

MING: I love you, too.

(*Pause.*)

OSCAR: Hold me.

(MING *goes to* OSCAR *and embraces him.*)

OSCAR: Close.

MING: Hmm.

OSCAR: Hold me close.

MING: Yeah.

OSCAR: Don't let go.

MING: Yeah.

OSCAR: Don't let go.

MING: I won't.

OSCAR: Don't let go.

MING: Shhh.

OSCAR: Don't let go. Don't let go. Don't let go.

(*Lights dim.*)

Broken English

OSCAR *and* MING *as they were in the last act.*

Despite the numerous scenes in this act, it should flow as fluidly as the prior act. All characters should remain on the set throughout.

MING: I can never forget what he said to me.

OSCAR: Hold me.

MING: Don't let go.

OSCAR: It seemed like an eternity.

MING: Us holding each other.

OSCAR: After a while, we broke away.

MING: Then Robert and I quickly left the party.

OSCAR: I saw both of them walking away. They made a handsome couple. We looked like that once. A long time ago.

MING: Walking beside me, Robert's mute eyes wrestled uncomfortably with the question of where I had earlier disappeared to. I squeezed Robert's hand. Deliberately. As if I was squeezing all his doubts away. And he smiled. That Robert smile. It was as if I never left him.

OSCAR: I saw Daniel. Sitting on an overcrowded couch with his friends. Holding court. I lingered near the couch and managed to catch snippets of their heated conversation. Government spending on AIDS. Racism within the gay community. Relationships. Madonna. Suddenly, I wanted to shout. At Daniel. Fuck off. You don't know what the fuck you're babbling about. Shut up. Shut up. Fuck off. Shut up. Fuck off. Then my head began to ring. Pound. Felt faint. Thirsty. Weak. Couldn't breathe.

MING: I agreed to move to L.A. With Robert. He thought the move was best. For him. For me. For us.

OSCAR: He never called. Not once. When I finally called—months later—a dull, lifeless, middle-aged female voice told me the number had been disconnected.

MING: Our belongings were already packed into little brown boxes. Phones disconnected. Mail forwarded.

OSCAR: In desperate disbelief, I kept dialing the same seven numbers over and over again. But her obstinate, mechanical voice never wavered from her prepared text. She didn't give me a clue to where he'd gone. A hint to what he was up to.

MING: Perhaps the reason I wanted to go to Oscar's party was to revisit the apartment where I spent four years of my life. To see Oscar's face one last time. To say good-bye to him. But I guess I didn't know the words to tell Oscar about leaving for L.A. About leaving him.

(ROBERT, *a Caucasian man in his late twenties, enters.*)

ROBERT: In three weeks we found ourselves a quaint, sun-kissed, Spanish stucco apartment overlooking the restless Pacific Ocean in a place called Venice.

(*Lights change.*)

MING: I see us

ROBERT: Paris in winter, hand in hand.

MING: I see us

ROBERT: Walking along frigid banks of River Seine.

MING: I see us

ROBERT: Not saying a word

MING: Laughing.

ROBERT: I see us

MING: Lost

ROBERT: In narrow streets of Florence.

MING: I see us

ROBERT: Walking along old bridge Vecchio

MING: Listening to lonely arias in adagio

ROBERT: In awe of shadows

MING: Cast in paintings by Caravaggio.

ROBERT: I see you

MING: Looking at me

ROBERT: Not saying a word

MING: Smiling.

ROBERT: I see us .

MING: Here in L.A.

ROBERT: Cooking pasta made like Mom's

MING: Listening to a sad violin by Brahms.

ROBERT: I see you

MING: Not saying a word

ROBERT: Thinking.

MING: I see us

ROBERT: Taking hot showers together

MING: His hands on me

ROBERT: His mind far away.

MING: I see us

ROBERT: On a lone pier

MING: Old couples on park benches with nothing to say

ROBERT: Young lovers at play

MING: Doves taking to the air, flying far, far away.

ROBERT: I see you

MING: Not saying a word

ROBERT: Contemplating.

MING: I see us

ROBERT: Sitting on expensive furniture

MING: In vast showrooms

ROBERT: On rainy Saturday afternoons.

MING: I see us

ROBERT: Not saying a word

MING: Sighing.

ROBERT: I see us

MING: In the comfort of a bed

ROBERT: Sunlight falling

MING: On bodies breathing.

ROBERT: I see you

MING: Silent

ROBERT: Not saying a word

MING: Frowning.

ROBERT: I see you

MING: Looking away

ROBERT: Not saying a word

MING: Wondering.

ROBERT: I see us.

MING: I see us.

ROBERT: I see us.

MING: I see us.

(MING *looks at* OSCAR.)

(*Lights change.*)

(DANIEL, *an Asian man in his early twenties, enters.*)

DANIEL: I thought it was high time to move off campus. It's one thing to bunk in with a hundred, heterosexual, horny, half-naked boys. It's another if I have to wait in line for the bathroom. Just to blow dry.

OSCAR: Of course—I suggested—that he should—move in with me.

DANIEL: He hinted that I move in. In so many words.

OSCAR: Danny—you can—you know—stay—move in—here—if you want.

DANIEL: You only have to read between the lines. If you want.

OSCAR: It was only proper. Given our circumstances. We were seeing each other.

DANIEL: Move in as roommates. Or move in as lovers?

OSCAR: I didn't know what to say.

DANIEL: Boyfriend wasn't ready. To make the leap.

OSCAR: I'm HIV positive. It's a different lifestyle.

DANIEL: Boyfriend has a disease. Called fear of commitment.

OSCAR: It's not about commitment. I love him—I do—I want to be with—want him—more than anything else in the world. I just don't want this to—come between—pry us apart. It'll strain—it's bad as it is—but living with someone who's positive—twenty-four hours a day—isn't easy. It's probably best—this way.

DANIEL: He thinks I'll leave. Like Ming. His ex.

OSCAR: So he went on a rampage looking for a place to call his own.

DANIEL: I don't need much.

OSCAR: A place that is quiet.

DANIEL: Comfortable.

OSCAR: Affordable.

DANIEL: Gay-friendly. Asian-friendly. Or just—friendly.

OSCAR: A Victorian brownstone building circa late 1800s.

DANIEL: No screaming children. No femmes with big hair.

OSCAR: Large bay windows with a view of trees. Like mine.

DANIEL: A stone's throw from the hairdresser's, gay bars, and a trendy outdoor cafe.

OSCAR: Hardwood floors. Exactly like the ones Ming and I used to—uh—walk on.

DANIEL: Cute security men wielding thick batons.

OSCAR: Heat and air-conditioning.

DANIEL: The basic necessities for an urban queer.

OSCAR: I was almost relieved when he said he wouldn't move in.

DANIEL: If I move in with him, and he's not ready, I'll be out on the streets. Back to square one. Looking for an apartment in three weeks. With my matching suitcases. Sans boyfriend.

OSCAR: I was actually a little offended when he said no.

DANIEL: Listen, I love him. Without a doubt. He's my first big love. But, to be practically honest, it's très difficult to live with someone who's HIV positive. Très, très, très high maintenance. You've got to watch your temper. Watch what you say. Be understanding. Be June Cleaver on a good hair day. And that's real tough when you feel more like Linda Blair with a chainsaw.

OSCAR: I mean, I want him here with me. But not all the time.

DANIEL: So I found a place close by.

OSCAR: He moved into a little apartment.

DANIEL: Across the street.

OSCAR: It's a comfortable distance.

(*Lights change.*)

(ROBERT *goes to* MING *and hugs him from behind.* MING *shrugs him off.*)

MING: Don't—

ROBERT: What?

MING: You always do that—

ROBERT: I thought you always liked—

MING: I did—just don't—

ROBERT: Listen, I got us—

MING: Tickets—

(ROBERT *fixes* MING's *clothes.*)

ROBERT: *Otello*—

MING: *Otello*—

ROBERT: It's the opera everyone's raving—

MING: Well, good—

(MING *shrugs* ROBERT *off.*)

ROBERT: The critics love—

MING: Okay, okay—

ROBERT: And right before the—

MING: No—

ROBERT: Cocktails with Jason and Tim—

MING: Not again—

ROBERT: Can you be nice?—

MING: Listen—

ROBERT: They're people we should get to—

MING: Robert—

ROBERT: Tim is an important—

MING: Robert—

ROBERT: Let's not fight over this—

MING: We should—talk.

ROBERT: Fine. But we're still going to—

MING: About other things.

ROBERT: I've been trying to bring you to operas, plays—

MING: I've been thinking—

ROBERT: Art exhibitions, books, magazines—

MING: I think—

ROBERT: And you always fight me—

MING: I think we should see other people.

ROBERT: What?

MING: I think—

ROBERT: Other people—

MING: You know—

ROBERT: See other people—

MING: Which means—

ROBERT: No.

(*Pause.*)

MING: No?

ROBERT: We are not seeing other people.

MING: I don't understand—

ROBERT: We're not—you can't—that's final—

MING: I don't think you—

ROBERT: Have you thought about this? Have you?

MING: Yes—

ROBERT: No, you haven't—

MING: Yes, I have—

ROBERT: Do you want to break up—

MING: No—

ROBERT: You want to leave—

MING: You're not listening—

ROBERT: This is exactly how my folks broke up—

MING: Let's not get into this again—

ROBERT: I wanted us to be different—

MING: Listen—

ROBERT: I can't believe this—

MING: We're not breaking up—

ROBERT: I thought we were perfect—happy—

MING: I'm not saying we should stop seeing—

ROBERT: No. Of course not.

MING: Nothing's going to change. Nothing.

ROBERT: Except you'll be seeing other people.

MING: It's not only me. You can—as well—

ROBERT: That's very generous.

MING: I think this will be good for us—

ROBERT: Good for you.

MING: For you. For us—

ROBERT: See other people. What's "see"?—

MING: You know what I mean—

ROBERT: To look?—

MING: Let's not—

ROBERT: Browse—stare—

MING: Robert—please—

ROBERT: Have coffee. Go to the movies. What?—

MING: Why are you doing this?—

ROBERT: To touch—to feel—to be with—

MING: To sleep with—to fuck with—okay?

(*Pause.*)

ROBERT (*softly*): Why?

MING: I am—

ROBERT: Bored.

MING: No. I am—

ROBERT: Suffocated.

MING: Stop finishing my sentences.

ROBERT: What did I do?

MING: Nothing.

ROBERT: What didn't I do?

MING: It's not you. It's me. Listen, I'm doing this to—

ROBERT: Hurt me—

MING: Would you rather I lied to you? Cheated on you?

ROBERT: Yes.

MING: Nothing will change.

ROBERT: Yeah.

MING: Between us. Really.

ROBERT: Yeah. Sure.

MING: What would you rather I—

ROBERT: I don't know.

MING: Tell me.

ROBERT: See other people.

MING: Are you sure?

ROBERT: No.

MING: I don't want to do this if you're—

ROBERT: Don't. Please. Just do it. And be careful.

MING: I will.

ROBERT: Hold me.

MING: Yeah.

(ROBERT *stands immobile as* MING *walks toward him.* MING *hugs* ROBERT.)

ROBERT: Tight.

MING: Yeah.

ROBERT: I love you.

MING: More than anything else in the world.

ROBERT: More than anything else in the world.

(*Lights change.*)

ROBERT:

    I have this glimpse of us
    Ming and me
    Sitting on a park bench
    Old and wrinkled
    Together holding hands
    Framed by naked, barren birch trees
    Invisible light rain, among golden crimson leaves
    Like the old couple in the park
    The couple we saw years ago when we first met
    And that image always lingered in corners of my mind
    It haunted me, excited me, in so many ways

    That old couple became a dream
    A glowing, beckoning dream within arm's reach
    A dream to be in love with that someone for eternity
    That friend, that lover, that soul mate
    That someone I've been dreaming of
    Ming

    That same dream became a nightmare
    An unattainable, unfathomable dream
    And with it, a crippling fear
    A fear that hot love and passion may simmer to its
      eventual cool
    A fear that he may be uncertain, unsure, of his feelings,
      his touch, his affection for me
    A fear that he may find someone else, and I, like light
      rain, dissolve, disappear from mind

A fear that he may leave, like all others before him, and I,
    back where I started, in the lonesome dark
A fear that I may find deliberate ways, unfair unkind, to
    cling desperate onto loose seams of my fractured
    dream
A fear that we may never be that old couple in the park

I have this glimpse
Of us

(*Lights change.*)

OSCAR: We spend all of our weekends at Ikea.

DANIEL: Not all. Every other weekend.

OSCAR: Glorious Ikea. The Swedish fix-it-yourself, discount-furniture megastore.

DANIEL: Possibly Sweden's biggest export since Abba and euthanasia.

OSCAR: He moved into a new apartment and tastefully decorated it according to pages 56 to 59 of the Ikea catalogue.

DANIEL: I spared no expense.

OSCAR: Instant homes. Affordable prices. If only relationships came that way.

DANIEL: The concept of instant homes was appealing and accessible. But assembling the furniture was another issue.

OSCAR: Building a home takes time. Each piece of furniture in the room should evoke a memory, a time, and the people that surrounded it. Furniture is sentimental. Not mass produced and instant.

DANIEL: We would spend hours—

OSCAR: Hours—

DANIEL: Looking at living room upon living room. One was done in black leather and cold steel that said "single-gay-Asian-workaholic-accountant-in-his-late-thirties-unable-to-have-emotional-relationships-a.k.a.-you-know-who."

OSCAR: We were making our second round of the showrooms.

DANIEL: Another had an oak and pine theme—très Heidi—dripping in Laura Ashley prints that screamed Republican virgin spinster or repressed male homosexual.

OSCAR: I was getting tired.

DANIEL: Then there was an Oriental rosewood and marble motif that told me to brew some jasmine and call the girls over for some serious mahjong. Très *Joy Luck Club*.

OSCAR: The place was getting crowded and hot.

DANIEL: And I still haven't made up my dizzy mind.

OSCAR: I felt achy.

DANIEL: Now, there's an interesting kitchen table. Très Quaker.

OSCAR: Suddenly, I realized Danny was gone. Nowhere to be found.

DANIEL: Love that couch.

OSCAR: Crowds of people.

DANIEL: The fabric design is so cubist.

OSCAR: People pushing. Shoving.

DANIEL: It speaks to me.

OSCAR: I feel hot. Sweaty.

DANIEL: It'd look fabulous with my Picasso print.

OSCAR: People talking. Toddlers shrieking.

DANIEL: But do I really want to look at that couch every time I'm in the living room?

OSCAR: I was lost. In a maze of showrooms. Like a child.

DANIEL: When I turned to Boyfriend to ask for his opinion, I discovered he was missing.

OSCAR: I started getting panicky.

DANIEL: Fuck.

OSCAR: Worried.

DANIEL: I looked around for him.

OSCAR: Started to push my way through the crowd.

DANIEL: No sign of him anywhere.

OSCAR: People got upset. Angry.

DANIEL: Where the fuck is he? Shit.

OSCAR: Suddenly my strength left me. I had no choice but to sit on the floor.

(OSCAR *sits on the floor.*)

DANIEL: I shouldn't have wandered. He shouldn't have wandered.

OSCAR: People looking at me. Concerned. Curious.

DANIEL: There was a crowd straight ahead.

OSCAR: Children laughing. Pointing their fingers at me.

DANIEL: Then I found him. Sitting in the middle of the floor. Looking like a desperate child who had lost his parents.

OSCAR: I wanted to die.

DANIEL: For a moment, I couldn't move. Couldn't push myself into the voyeuristic crowd to help him. Instead, I stood there. Paralyzed. With fascination. Watching him. Sitting on the floor. As if he were a stranger. Someone I didn't know. Someone I didn't care for. Someone I could leave behind at a moment's notice.

OSCAR: I started crying.

DANIEL: After a while, I broke through the crowd and moved toward him.

(DANIEL *goes over to* OSCAR *and helps him up.* OSCAR *holds* DANIEL *tightly.*)

OSCAR: Danny?

DANIEL: Baby.

OSCAR (*scoldingly*): Don't leave me.

DANIEL: It's okay. It's okay. Let's go home.

(*Lights change.*)

MING:
I receive Randy's message on my voice mail
I hear him say, "Same place at one"
I drive, in the blistering heat, as if given a command
I'm half shaking with anticipation, half annoyed at his
    barking message

I arrive, in a bathhouse, in Hollywood
I get myself a locker
I wrap myself with a white towel, smelling faintly of
    bleach
I walk barefoot to our usual room, at the end of the floor
I see him there, lying on a narrow bed, with a half-open door
I see him, naked, stroking himself, smoking a
    Marlborough
I think of Robert, most afternoons, in a bathhouse,
    in Hollywood

I'm greeted by Randy's hungry wet kisses
I feel his urgent tongue forcing down my throat
I push his hot body onto the bed, grabbing his hairy legs
    tightly
I hoist them angrily into the air, his head buried in a
    soft pillow
I enter him forcefully, ignoring his welcoming whimpers
I fuck him ruthlessly, punishing him for his halting voice
    mail, thinking I'm his secretary in his office, his
    curt orders I shamelessly follow
I grab his hard dick, fucking him, slowly, gently
I feel his tight warmth, fucking him, sturdily, steadily
I hear him grunt in pain and sensation, fucking him,
    harder and harder, with abandon
I think about Oscar, wondering how he is, fucking him
    cruelly
I think about why I'm here, why I'm doing this, fucking
    him, feeling weak, feeling close
I think about the countless strangers I've made love to in
    this narrow room, fucking him, exploding, biting
    his neck, screaming

I think about Robert, most afternoons, in a bathhouse, in
   Hollywood

I see Randy, walking away, to the sound of roaring
   showers
I wonder if his wife knows about him, me, us
I think about my habit of meeting strangers in white
   towels, in the flickering, dim light of my room
I enjoy the welcome anonymity, the immediate
   urge to possess these men, to make love to them
I bask in the comfort of their silence, making love without
   uttering a word, leaving without a sound
I'm always struck by the immediate emptiness and
   disappointment, once the love is made, once the
   door is again shut
I notice how my cavalier, silent lovers seem to look like
   Oscar, how they smell like him, how they feel like
   him
I make love to them the way I made love to Oscar
I wonder if they like me, love me, need me
I wonder if they feel anything for me

I think this, as a nameless man in half light looks at me,
   nodding
I think this, as he drowns me in a sea of hot kisses, his
   fingers, touching me, there
I think this, as he gets on his knees, his head against my
   aching groin, his warm mouth, there
I think this, my head arching back, against a wall, my eyes
   closed
I think of Robert, most afternoons, in a bathhouse, in
   Hollywood

(*Pause.*)

MING: So?

ROBERT: Look, I didn't plan it—

MING: Didn't plan it—

ROBERT: It was a spur of the moment thing—

MING: Spur of the moment—

ROBERT: I didn't plan it—I didn't think, okay? Look, I thought you were at the gym—

MING: You must think—

ROBERT: Otherwise I wouldn't have—

MING: What's your point?

ROBERT: Wait a minute.

MING: Who's the one fucking in our bedroom?—

ROBERT: Don't you fucking put the blame on me— Don't—

MING: On our bed? With what's his name—

ROBERT: Pran—

MING: Him. Again—

ROBERT: I didn't plan this—

MING: I think you did—

ROBERT: I didn't—it wasn't deliberate—it just—

MING: I don't care—

ROBERT: You were the one—

MING: Don't. You always use that against me—

ROBERT: See other people. You were the one who said—

MING: But didn't we agree—

ROBERT: Expand our horizons, you said—

MING: Didn't we agree we shouldn't do it in our apartment—

ROBERT: So I slipped— Oops—

MING: Slipped—

ROBERT: Now what do you want me to do? Beg? Beg for your forgiveness? What?—

MING: You broke our—

ROBERT: We were just watching TV, and it just—

MING: It doesn't matter. I thought this arrangement would be a good thing—

ROBERT: I just went along with it—

MING: Willingly. You went along—

ROBERT: Get real. The real reason you're upset with me isn't that I'm on our bed fucking. You're upset I'm fucking Pran, aren't you? The guy I'm always with. Not like one of your one-night stands.

MING: I don't know what you're—

ROBERT: Let me put this in plain and simple English. You're jealous.

MING: Jealous? Of that little Vietnamese boat person? I don't give a—

ROBERT: Obviously, you do.

MING: I don't.

ROBERT: You're upset because I keep seeing him. Spending time with him.

(ROBERT *tweaks* MING's *nipple.*)

MING: I'm not—stop it—

ROBERT: I keep seeing him. And you keep seeing other guys—

(ROBERT *plays with* MING's *hair.*)

MING: I said stop it—

ROBERT: Says something about you, doesn't it?—

MING: That's enough—

ROBERT: You just can't deal with the fact that Pran likes me—

(ROBERT *kisses* MING's *neck.*)

MING: He what?

ROBERT: He likes me.

(ROBERT *gently nibbles on* MING's *ear.*)

MING: Really?

ROBERT: Yeah. He likes me.

(ROBERT *touches* MING's *face.*)

MING: He likes you.

ROBERT: He likes me.

(ROBERT *flirtatiously touches* MING*'s chest.*)

ROBERT: He likes me.

(ROBERT *sits on* MING*'s lap.* ROBERT *grabs* MING*'s crotch.*)

ROBERT: He likes me.

(MING *suddenly lurches toward* ROBERT *and slaps him hard in the face. He punches him twice. Suddenly, as if exhausted or shocked, he stops dumbfoundedly, staring blankly at* ROBERT. *On the ground,* ROBERT *winces in pain and surprise. When* MING *realizes what he has done, he reaches out for* ROBERT. ROBERT, *thinking* MING *is about to assault him again, shies away. Remorsefully,* MING *hugs* ROBERT *tight. A beat later.*)

MING: I—love you—

ROBERT: Yeah. (*A beat.*) More than anything else in the world.

(ROBERT *looks longingly at* MING. MING *kisses* ROBERT. *Urgently,* ROBERT *responds.*)

(*Lights change.*)

(OSCAR *looks at* MING.)

OSCAR: I love you.

DANIEL: Three little words.

(OSCAR *looks at* DANIEL.)

OSCAR: I love you.

DANIEL: He says to me.

OSCAR: I love you.

DANIEL: Every moment of the day.

OSCAR: I love you.

DANIEL: All the time.

OSCAR: I love you.

DANIEL: Unceasingly.

OSCAR: I love you.

DANIEL: His affection never wanting.

OSCAR: I love you.

DANIEL: He always touches me.

OSCAR: I love you.

DANIEL: Holds me. Hugs me. Kisses me.

OSCAR: I love you.

DANIEL: On crowded street corners. On subway trains. On kitchen floors.

OSCAR: I love you.

DANIEL: I hear it.

OSCAR: I love you.

DANIEL: He says. He whispers. He shouts.

OSCAR: I love you.

DANIEL: In the throes of love. Under duvet covers. Flat on my back.

OSCAR: I love you.

DANIEL: On the rinse cycle. With my mud mask. Aerobizing. To Whitney.

OSCAR: I love you.

DANIEL: I never tire of these words.

OSCAR: I love you.

DANIEL: Not really. Really.

OSCAR: I love you.

DANIEL: It's what I breathe for. What I live for. What I die for.

OSCAR: I love you.

DANIEL: It's—music—to my—you know—

OSCAR: I love you.

DANIEL: I never want him to—stop—not really—

OSCAR: I love you.

DANIEL: I wonder if he means it. What he says.

OSCAR: I love you.

DANIEL: I wonder if he's cheating on me. Hiding something.

OSCAR: I love you.

DANIEL: I wonder what "love" means—translated in Chinese.

OSCAR: I love you.

DANIEL: I wonder if that's his way. The way they do it in China or wherever he's from.

OSCAR: I love you.

DANIEL: It's delightful. Nice. It's driving me insane.

OSCAR: I love you.

DANIEL: I wish he'd stop. I thought all Asian men were typically quiet.

OSCAR: I love you.

DANIEL: Three little words.

OSCAR: I love you.

DANIEL: He says to me.

OSCAR: I love you.

DANIEL: All the time.

OSCAR: I love you.

DANIEL: Unceasingly.

OSCAR: I love you.

DANIEL: Cease it.

(*Lights change.*)

(*At one corner of the stage,* OSCAR *wakes up with a start.*)

OSCAR: Danny? Danny? Danny! Danny! Danny!

(DANIEL *goes to* OSCAR.)

DANIEL: Yes?

OSCAR: Where were you?

DANIEL: Outside. I was—

OSCAR: Where were—

DANIEL: Here. I'm here.

OSCAR: Don't—don't do that—

DANIEL: I won't.

OSCAR: Don't leave—without—

DANIEL: Are you okay?

OSCAR: Don't ever do that again!

(In another corner, MING *and* ROBERT *attempt to make love.)*

MING: I'm sorry.

ROBERT: It's okay.

MING: I guess I'm just—

ROBERT: Yeah.

MING: I really want to—you know—

ROBERT: I know.

MING: Do you want to—?

ROBERT: No. It's okay.

(In OSCAR*'s corner.)*

DANIEL: Another bad dream?

OSCAR: Yes. Struggling. Fighting. Running.

DANIEL: Running from?

OSCAR: Just running. Like I was being chased.

DANIEL: Where?

OSCAR: Don't know. In some shopping mall.

DANIEL: Ikea?

OSCAR: No. You weren't in the dream.

(*In* MING's *corner.*)

MING: I'm sorry about— You get me so—

ROBERT: Upset.

MING: The things I want to say—

ROBERT: Come out—

MING: Yes. Like this. The words—thoughts—it's—

ROBERT: Difficult.

(*In* OSCAR's *corner.*)

OSCAR: Funny. All my dreams. I'm always chasing or being chased.

DANIEL: Freudian.

OSCAR: Never once—flying.

DANIEL: You've never? It's a great feeling. You feel so free. Like a bird. Like a maxi-pad commercial. It feels just like that.

OSCAR: I wish I could— (OSCAR *groans.*)

(*In* MING's *corner.* MING *slowly and delicately touches the bruise on* ROBERT's *face.*)

MING: Does it—?

ROBERT: No.

MING: Really?

ROBERT: I'm fine.

(*In* OSCAR's *corner.*)

DANIEL: What's wrong?

OSCAR: I feel—

DANIEL: Sick?

OSCAR: Weak.

DANIEL: I'll call the doctor.

OSCAR: It's okay. Just queasy. Wiped out.

(*In* MING's *corner.*)

MING: It won't happen again. You know that. It won't happen
 again.

ROBERT: No. It won't.

MING: Promise.

ROBERT: Yeah.

(*In* OSCAR's *corner.* OSCAR *grimaces in pain. When* DANIEL *reaches
for* OSCAR's *hand,* OSCAR *grabs* DANIEL's *finger. Holds it tightly.*)

DANIEL: Better?

OSCAR: No. But it'll be better.

DANIEL: Sure?

OSCAR: Sure.

(*A beat.*)

DANIEL: You're holding my finger.

(*In* MING's *corner.*)

MING: I—love you.

ROBERT: I love you, too.

MING: More than anything else in the world.

ROBERT: More than anything else in the world.

(ROBERT *kisses* MING *tenderly.*)

(*Lights change.*)

DANIEL: I know I'm not perfect. But you know what gets my dander up? It seems that Boyfriend always has the perfect reason to be upset. Throwing random tantrums because he's sick. And if I get into a hissy fit, especially during that time of the month, I'm Bette Davis serving din-dins on a silver platter. So maybe he has a better reason. But being Dear Abby all the time isn't easy.

ROBERT: I know what I want isn't easy. I know my dream of a perfect relationship is difficult to obtain. I know it's a fantasy to want the kind of life prescribed by Judith Krantz paperback novels and misty black-and-white movies. I know. But I know I can have it. I know we just have to try a little harder, Ming has to try a little harder. I know this relationship is what I want, it's what Ming wants. I know things aren't perfect now, but we'll be perfect, he'll be perfect.

DANIEL: Our très sincere friends always mince up to me and ask me about Boyfriend. "How is he doing?" "Is the poor dear okay?" "Does he want to watch *My Fair Lady* again?" Like he's dying. Like he's Camille. Meanwhile, Boyfriend looks fine. Looks perfect. Not a hair out of place. Never felt better. Smiling like he's just got laid by Fabio. He's fine. Fine.

ROBERT: We're still in love. We're still in a relationship. We still go to the opera. We still have quiet dinners at only the best restaurants. We still spend long weekends with interesting people doing interesting things. We still take spontaneous exotic trips to faraway places where a word of English is never spoken. We're fine. Perfect. We are. We are.

DANIEL: So it's not perfect all the time. Sometimes life can be difficult with Boyfriend. It's hard to care for him. To be around him. His moods. Sometimes I wonder why I'm here. And sometimes I get a little emotional. Cry in the middle of the day. Wondering what it's like without Boyfriend. Don't know why. Sometimes I just blank. Get angry. Depressed. Sometimes I— I just—just—I'm fine. Really. Fine.

ROBERT: You see other people. You come home late. You kiss me. You buy me gifts. You go to bed. You sleep. You smell of someone's cologne. You give me things. You see other people. You give me money. You take me on trips. You see other people. You take me to expensive restaurants. You give me your credit card. You see other people. You know I love you. You know I'll never leave you. You see other people. You know I need you. You know I need what you give me. You know I need you more than you need me. You see other people. You know it's perfect.

DANIEL: Sometimes I spend a thoughtless hour or two with a nameless man. Slipping into another world that could have been Boyfriend's and mine. A world without AIDS or death. Just the two of us. Happy. Together. And after the passion between two strangers is spent, I'm back in the same living room with unsuspecting Boyfriend. Feeling a little guilty. A little renewed. A little hopeful. A little fine.

ROBERT: I wonder if my dream of a perfect relationship is just that. A dream, a stupid dream. I wonder if I will ever find that special someone. I wonder if that special someone is him. I wonder if I'll lose that special someone in the crowd if I stay too long with him. I wonder if I'm always on his mind. I wonder if he wants me, needs me, loves me. I wonder if he feels the same way I do. I wonder if he sees through all my careless imperfections. I wonder if someone else can love him more than I can. I wonder if someone else can love me more than he can.

DANIEL: No one asks how I'm doing. Everyone assumes. That I'm fine. And I am. Fine. For a while. Fine. I try to be. I have to be. Fine. And, of course, after softening my luscious cheeks with Pearl Cream, I'll look better than fine. I knew this relationship was going to be hard. Going into it. And somehow I thought it'd be a little easier. Because Boyfriend's the one, you know. The only one for me. And that—keeps me going.

(DANIEL *and* ROBERT *look at each other for a brief moment.*)

(*Lights change.*)

(*In* MING's *corner.*)

ROBERT: I don't think we should see each other anymore—

MING: What?

ROBERT: It's for the best—

MING: Why?—

ROBERT: It's not working—

MING: You're in love with—

ROBERT: That's not the point—

MING: That Vietcong—

ROBERT: Don't—

MING: I thought you said we should talk—

ROBERT: I did but—

MING: Let's talk—

ROBERT: It's too late.

(*In* OSCAR's *corner.* OSCAR *slow dances with* DANIEL.)

DANIEL: Dancing.

OSCAR: Like we used to. In the living room.

DANIEL: Yes. I missed this.

OSCAR: Me, too. (*They kiss.*)

(*In* MING's *corner.*)

ROBERT: I'm going to stay with—

MING: That boat person—

ROBERT: You're so incredibly—

MING: You planned this, didn't you?

ROBERT: Racist—it's amazing that—

MING: Like you always did—scheming—plotting—

ROBERT: Is it so difficult to remember his—

MING: It slips my mind—

ROBERT: Pran—

MING: You always clam up when—

ROBERT: I don't want to talk about him—

MING: I want to—

ROBERT: Why? There's nothing to—

MING: I'm not asking for intimate—

ROBERT: Hey, I don't ask what you do—

MING: I'll tell you if you want to know.

(*In* OSCAR's *corner.* OSCAR *and* DANIEL *dance. Suddenly,* OSCAR *winces in pain.*)

DANIEL: What's wrong?

OSCAR: Pain. Shooting pains.

DANIEL: Where—the pain— (OSCAR *falls to the ground.*)

(*In* MING's *corner.*)

ROBERT: Drop it. You're acting like a child—

MING: You're so full of secrets.

ROBERT: I'm going. To Pran. I'm staying with him.

(*Overlapping with* MING *and* ROBERT.)

DANIEL: You've got to hold on.

OSCAR: In my—stomach.

DANIEL: Let me get your—

OSCAR: It won't help.

DANIEL: Here.

OSCAR: No, it hurts.

DANIEL: Think about something else. It'll help. Anything. I don't know.

MING: Maybe you like to finish his sentences too. Correct his English. Don't you think it's so cute when he calls? (*Mimics.*) "Hello, can I please speak to Robert?"

ROBERT: I'll leave his number on the table in case—

MING: No!

(OSCAR *looks at* MING.)

OSCAR: Ming?

(MING *looks at* OSCAR. *They look at each other for the first time in this act. A beat later.*)

DANIEL: Daniel.

(OSCAR *turns his glance to Daniel.* MING *looks at* ROBERT.)

OSCAR: What?

DANIEL: Nothing.

(*In* MING's *corner.*)

MING: So what do you do with your evenings together? Practice English?—

ROBERT: Leave me alone—

(*In* OSCAR's *corner.*)

OSCAR: You've got to help me.

DANIEL: Yes. Anything.

OSCAR: I need some—sleeping pills.

DANIEL: Sleep. I'll get you a Valium from—

OSCAR: No! Not one. A lot.

(*In* MING's *corner.*)

MING: You love it, don't you? This white superiority—

ROBERT: He talks to me, asshole! With the few fucking English words he knows! In his broken English unbearable to your ears! He fucking talks to me! Not like you! I hate you!

(*In* OSCAR's *corner.*)

DANIEL: It's not what—

OSCAR: I know.

DANIEL: We said—

OSCAR: Fight it to the end.

DANIEL: But now—

OSCAR: You're not fighting it. I am.

(*In* MING's *corner.* MING *grabs* ROBERT *by the neck and passionately kisses him.* ROBERT *responds.*)

MING: You love me. You need me.

(*In* OSCAR's *corner.*)

DANIEL: What about me? What about me?

OSCAR: I don't care! (*Pause.*) I mean—

DANIEL: I know. Really.

(*In* MING's *corner.* ROBERT *breaks away from* MING's *kiss.*)

ROBERT: I don't love you.

MING: Leave then.

(MING *strikes* ROBERT *across the face. With a sudden burst of strength,* ROBERT *lunges for a surprised* MING. ROBERT *decks him hard.* MING *does not retaliate, numbly accepting each blow.*)

ROBERT: I'm sick of you. Sick of you hitting me.

(*A beat.*)

ROBERT: Oh my god. I've become you.

(*In* OSCAR's *corner.*)

OSCAR: I'm dying.

DANIEL: No. You have to fight—

OSCAR: You promised. Promised to do anything for me.

DANIEL: But not this—I don't know—

OSCAR: Please.

DANIEL: Oh god. I don't know. I don't know. I don't know.

(*Lights change.*)
ROBERT:
In the beginning of our relationship, we learned each
  other's language
Like overeager babies
Mouthing unintelligible gaggles and sounds
Unable to articulate
Clumsily tripping on words
Falling into abject frustration
But once we found the common language
Each action and deed, every word and sentence was a joy,
  and an excitement
A tingling of senses
A radiant discovery

Then, as if through osmosis, we used each other's words
  and expressions
Borrowing shamelessly and
Indeliberately incorporating them into our language
Speaking as one
Thinking as one
Feeling as one
And in the course, we invented new words
Gave existing words new meaning
Redefined and polished our language
Making it a special one of our own
One that we selfishly shared
One that no one could decipher or understand
One that we used in the comfort of each other's arms in
  quiet evenings

Then we tired of it
Lost interest
Got lazy
Became indifferent
Words gradually lost their meaning and significance
Like drunken dancers, we emphasized wrong accents in
   words
Sentences led to misinterpretations
Misinterpretations led to misunderstandings
Misunderstandings led to inevitable silence

In the end, we spoke different languages

MING: Even though, we wanted the same thing.

(MING *looks at* ROBERT. *Unable to look at him,* ROBERT *walks away.*)

(*Lights change.*)

DANIEL: I—don't want to do this.

OSCAR: I know.

DANIEL: Don't want you to—

OSCAR: Yes.

DANIEL: How—how are you feeling?

OSCAR: The same.

DANIEL: Is it—helping?

OSCAR: Slowly.

DANIEL: Good.

OSCAR: You knew it'd come to this—

DANIEL: Yes, but—

OSCAR: Me leaving.

DANIEL: Leaving. Yes. I know.

OSCAR: If the hospital finds out—

DANIEL: I'll say I can't read English or something—

OSCAR: Say I did—

DANIEL: Misread the prescription on the bottle—

OSCAR: Say I wanted it—

DANIEL: I'll think of something.

OSCAR: We make a great team.

DANIEL: Yes. A great team.

OSCAR: Danny?

DANIEL: Yes?

OSCAR: I really appreciated everything—

DANIEL: I know.

OSCAR: Everything we did. Everything I put you through—

DANIEL: Do you love me?

OSCAR: What kind of question is that?

DANIEL: I don't know. Do you love me?

OSCAR: Of course. Yes.

DANIEL: I love you, too.

OSCAR: I know. So what are you going to do? With yourself. Once I–go.

DANIEL: Well, there's a fire sale at Ikea in the Whitelands Mall. So if you can kick off within the next half hour–

OSCAR: You always make me laugh.

DANIEL: You wouldn't if you knew I was charging that très–that très–

(*Pause.*)

OSCAR: Live.

DANIEL: What?

OSCAR: I want you to live.

DANIEL: Well, I don't feel much like it at the moment. Living. Live. (*A beat.*) I think I'm supposed to be the one to tell you that.

OSCAR: I'm sorry–

DANIEL: I want to say–say–I don't know what I want to say–there are so many things–and I can't–so many things but–

OSCAR: I know.

DANIEL: I want to grow old with you. I want to always hear your voice. I want to dance with you. Like we used to. Every night. To Satie.

OSCAR: Me too.

DANIEL: I want to–so many things.

OSCAR: I know. You knew this would come.

DANIEL: Don't leave me. Please.

OSCAR: I think I'll miss you very much. (*A beat.*) Why?

DANIEL: Why what?

OSCAR: Why did you get involved knowing that—

DANIEL: I think you know why.

(*A beat.*)

OSCAR: Say good-bye.

DANIEL: What?

OSCAR: It'll be easier.

DANIEL: I want to stay. With you.

OSCAR: Go.

DANIEL: Please.

OSCAR: I love you. (*A beat.*) Go.

DANIEL: No.

OSCAR: Go. Get a drink of water. Around the corner.

DANIEL: Why are you—

OSCAR: I need some time alone.

DANIEL: Why?

OSCAR: Remember. Live.

(DANIEL *looks at* OSCAR *for a long moment. Suddenly, he gets up and leaves. A beat later,* MING *comes into the room.*)

OSCAR: You are here.

MING: I never left.

OSCAR: Will you hold my hand?

MING: Yes.

OSCAR: It's getting a little colder.

MING: Do you want me to get you a blanket?

OSCAR: No. Hold my hand. Hold. Hold my finger.

MING: Your finger.

OSCAR: Yes. Like that. Yes. You used to hold it like that.

MING: Yes.

OSCAR: On trains. In streets.

MING: Listen—

OSCAR: Uh-huh—

MING: I'm sorry about how we—

OSCAR: Me too.

MING: I wish we could—

OSCAR: Yes. I wish—

MING: Wishing seems a little—

OSCAR: Never too late—

MING: You know I—

OSCAR: Yes. I love you, too.

MING: Me too.

OSCAR: You know—I always saw your face—everywhere I turned—felt you were always with me—

MING: I wish—

OSCAR: Shh—I know—

MING: You okay?

OSCAR: Yes. Fading. Feel like I'm—

MING: What?

OSCAR: Flying.

MING: Flying?

OSCAR: Higher and higher—

MING: Don't.

OSCAR: Have to—got to—flying—it's so—

MING: Liberating?

(*A beat.*)

OSCAR: Let go.

MING: What?

OSCAR: Let go.

MING: Of your finger?

OSCAR: Yes.

MING: No.

OSCAR: Need to fly.

MING: Fly.

OSCAR: Yes.

MING: Fly.

OSCAR: Fly.

MING: You're free.

OSCAR: Yes. Free. Free. Free. I'm flying.

(*Lights change.*)

MING: I heard he died alone in a sterile hospital room, overlooking the Charles River on a winter day.

DANIEL: After I took a drink at the water fountain, I stole back into Oscar's room and sat by his bed. He was breathing heavily. Choking. Mumbling. When I rested my hand on his—he suddenly grabbed my finger, As if by instinct. Holding it. Tightly. As if he knew it was me. Then he let go. He was gone.

MING: He's gone. That's what Daniel said. On the phone machine. Gone. Passed on. Whatever. We always have such nice words for terrible things. It was as if he was someone temporary. Someone we were never meant to have. To keep and to hold. Someone never meant to stay too long.

DANIEL: He was the first person I called. I just thought he should know. Ming would have wanted to be there. By his side.

MING: It was two years since I last saw Oscar. Two years. In a drafty bedroom upstairs. A rowdy party down below. Now, I'll never see his face again.

DANIEL: Later, I left him another message. Telling him where and when the service was going to be. In a church in the South End.

MING: I called back and said I'd be there.

DANIEL: We waited for about an hour before starting the service. But he never showed up.

MING: Of course—I would have been there—really—I would—if—but—I don't know. I wanted to but—I didn't—

DANIEL: When I got back to the apartment, there was a message on my machine. It was him. Saying that something had come up. Suddenly. Last minute. Couldn't make it. Hope it went well. That's what he said. Hope it went well.

MING: I remember telling him regardless of what happened, I would be there for him. I promised him. I did. And I would have, you know. Really. Now all I've said—it's just words. Empty words.

DANIEL: He didn't return my calls. The bastard would not return my calls.

MING: Daniel and I never really knew each other. All we could ever talk about was him. I didn't call him back.

DANIEL: I tried calling and calling. Leaving messages and—finally, I gave up. Perhaps, silence is best.

(*Lights change.*)

MING: I can never forget what he said to me.

OSCAR: Hold my finger.

MING: Like this?

OSCAR: Let go. Let go.

MING: I can't.

OSCAR: You have to.

MING: They say you always remember your first love.

OSCAR: You were mine, too.

MING: I wanted to grow old with you.

OSCAR: Yes.

(MING *breaks down and cries.*)

MING: Every day, the image of you grows dimmer in my mind. Like castles made of sand. With each oncoming tide, a little bit of the castle washes away. Until there's nothing left. I've forgotten what you look like.

OSCAR: It's okay.

MING: Forgotten what you smell like. What you sound like. What you taste like. I don't want to lose that.

OSCAR: You'll find new sounds. New smells.

DANIEL: I can never forget what he said to me.

OSCAR: Live.

DANIEL: Things haven't been the same without you.

OSCAR: How are you, Danny?

DANIEL: Okay.

OSCAR: Dating?

DANIEL: No. Organizing your things. Disconnecting your phone. Packing. Your things. Into little brown boxes. I hope you don't mind, but I'm giving most of it away to the AIDS project and the Salvation Army.

OSCAR: I don't mind.

DANIEL: I'm going to keep a few things. A few things that remind me of us.

OSCAR: The gray scarf you bought me last fall.

DANIEL: It still smells of you.

OSCAR: The Donna Summer CDs.

DANIEL: And Satie. Don't forget Satie. We used to—

OSCAR: Yes. And some pieces of furniture that hold history. Our history.

DANIEL: Sometimes I see you sitting on them.

OSCAR: How have you been?

DANIEL: Good. (*Pause.*) I'm positive.

OSCAR: No.

DANIEL: But I'm keeping healthy. Making cardboard-tasting, protein vegetable shakes. Bought a Cuisinart with your credit card at Neiman's.

OSCAR: You could have gotten it cheaper at Kmart.

DANIEL: I spared no expense.

OSCAR: I thought we were safe.

DANIEL: We were. It's probably not you. Perhaps someone before. Someone after. I don't know. The point is I'm positive.

OSCAR: Oh, Danny.

DANIEL: I'll be fine.

OSCAR: I wish I could do something for you, like what you did—

DANIEL: I'll be fine. Really. (*A beat.*) I miss you. Very much.

OSCAR: Me, too.

ROBERT: I can never forget what he said to me.

MING: I think we should—get together—meet—something—

ROBERT: Coffee?

MING: Yeah.

ROBERT: So—

MING: I have been thinking about you.

ROBERT: So have I.

MING: I want us to see each other again.

ROBERT: Uh-huh.

MING: You're not thrilled. You're seeing someone. Pran.

ROBERT: No. I am. Thrilled. I mean, I'm not seeing—it's all over with Pran. (*A beat.*) I just want it to be right, you know?

MING: Me, too. (*A beat.*) I've been getting help. With the—

ROBERT: Good. (*Pause.*) So—

MING: Coffee?

ROBERT: Dinner.

MING: Movie.

ROBERT: Revival?

MING: Sure. Sounds great.

(*Pause.*)

ROBERT: Listen.

MING: What?

ROBERT: I want to say—

MING: Yes?

ROBERT: I—I still—still—

(*A beat.*)

MING: I know. I know.

End of Play.

Acknowledgments

Since theater is a highly collaborative art, there are many remarkable individuals to whom I'm greatly indebted:

George C. Wolfe, for his unwavering encouragement, his lesson of breathing dragons, and for always championing brave new voices in American theater, especially in a climate where diversity and art are presently threatened.

Shelby Jiggetts, dramaturg and friend, for her unceasing questions and love.

Ong Keng Sen, for the very special moment when we stood outside the Public Theater on opening night after a long journey from the stages of Anglo-Chinese School and TheatreWorks in Singapore. I deeply appreciate his challenges, vision, and friendship.

Glen Goei, without whom I'd not have written *Porcelain*, for his firm belief and generosity, and for never saying no. I can never thank him enough.

David Drake, Dennis Dun, Radmar Jao, Francis Jue, Alec Mapa, Steve Park, Eric Steinberg, Garrett Wang, and B. D. Wong, the immensely talented actors, for breathing life into my words.

Rosemary Tichler, Myunghee Cho, Scott Zielinski, Buzz Cohen, and everyone at the Public Theater; Tim Dang and the entire East West Players; Robert Menna, Daniel Renner, and the Intiman Theatre; Gordon Davidson, Oskar Eustis, and the Mark Taper Forum; John Lee and Mu-Lan Theatre Company for their invaluable talent, support, and work on the development and production of *Porcelain* and *Language*.

George Lane and Jason Fogelson at William Morris for all their hard work, and for always returning my calls.

| 229

Kenn Russell for making this book a reality.

All my peers and friends, especially Luis Alfaro, Kevin Angle, Henry Wolfgang Carter, Randy Cupp, Bekah Dannelly, Timothy Douglas, Steve Ferger, Tod Morehead, Ben Pesner, Lisa Peterson, Sonja Piper, Diane Rodriguez, and Young Kong Shin for their infinite laughter, patience, and friendship throughout the entire process.

Scott Forbes for inspiring *Language* and G. Peter Schiller for leading me to *Porcelain*.

Finally, my parents, Kok Fun and Jennifer, for everything.

CPSIA information can be obtained
at www.ICGtesting.com
Printed in the USA
JSHW081712060723
44316JS00002B/23